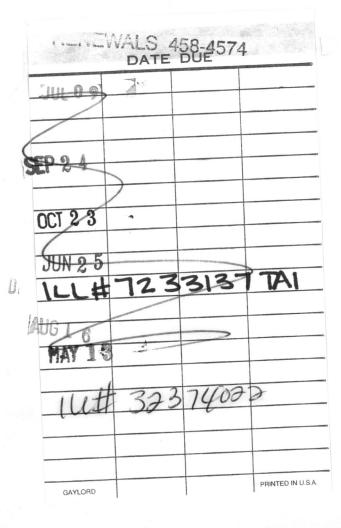

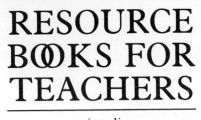

RESOURCE
BOOKS FOR
TEACHERS

series editor
ALAN MALEY

WRITING

Tricia Hedge

Oxford University Press

Oxford University Press
Walton Street, Oxford OX2 6DP

*Oxford   New York   Toronto
Delhi   Bombay   Calcutta   Madras   Karachi
Petaling Jaya   Singapore   Hong Kong   Tokyo
Nairobi   Dar es Salaam   Cape Town
Melbourne   Auckland*

and associated companies in
Berlin   Ibadan

Oxford and *Oxford English* are trade marks of
Oxford University Press

ISBN 0 19 437098 4

© Oxford University Press 1988
First published 1988
Fourth impression 1991

Set by Pentacor Ltd, High Wycombe, Bucks

Printed in Hong Kong

Acknowledgements

The publisher would like to thank the following for their permission to use copyright material:

Cambridge University Press (for an extract from 'The London region' in *Great Britain: Geographical Essays*, by M.J. Wise); Collins Publishers (for 'The legend of Alderley' from *The Weirdstone of Brisingamen*, by Alan Garner); Friends of the Earth (for 'Renewable energy'); Harper and Row (for 'First day' in *Black Boy*, by Richard Wright, and for US and Canada rights to use material from *Children Solve Problems*, by Edward de Bono); Heinemann Educational Books Ltd (for the diagram from *Writing and the Writer*, by Frank Smith); Joint Matriculation Board (for samples of examination papers from Test in English (Overseas)); Macmillan Publishers Ltd (for extracts from *The River Thames Guidebook*, and *Using Readers in the Language Classroom*, by Tricia Hedge); Thomas Nelson and Sons Ltd (for an extract from *Freestyle* by Tricia Hedge); Oxford and County Newspapers (for 'It's me, Dad!', *The Oxford Star*, 16 April 1987, and 'Daughter's voice "saved my life"', *The Oxford Times*, 17 April 1987); Penguin Books Ltd (for extracts 'A wife's thoughts III', 'In imitation of "Since you, sir, went away"', and 'In imitation of Hsü Kan' in *The Penguin Book of Chinese Verse*, translated by Robert Kotewall and Norman L. Smith, and for three illustrations from *Children Solve Problems* by Edward de Bono); Royal Society of Arts (for an extract from *Communicative Use of English as a Foreign Language*).

The publisher would also like to thank the following Oxford University Press authors for agreeing to reproduction of their material:

L.A. Hill (for an extract from *Writing for a Purpose*); M. Rinvolucri (for the letter from *ELT Journal*, Vol 37/1); W. Tevis and D. Fickling (for the collage from *The Man Who Fell to Earth* (adapted)).

Illustrations by:

Phil Gascoine, Kevin Jones Associates, and Kim Raymond

Location photography by:

Rob Judges and John Ramussen

The publisher would like to thank the following for their permission to reproduce photographs:

Format, HDM Horner Collis & Kisvan, and Network

The publisher has been unable to trace the following copyright holders and would like to hear from them:

Paul Turner (translator of 'Moon people' from Lucian: *Satyrical Sketches*, Penguin Classics, 1961); Nuclear Information (extract from their leaflet 'Nuclear power: the facts').

Contents

2 Communicating

The author and series editor

Tricia Hedge began her teaching career in Britain, teaching English to mother tongue and second language learners in secondary schools. She then spent many years in Sweden where, as Head of the Extra Mural English Department of Uppsala University, she organized general purpose and ESP courses, trained teachers, designed materials, and taught adults and adolescents. She is now a Principal Lecturer in the EFL/ESL Division of the School of Language Studies at Ealing College of Higher Education in London. She runs the MA in English Language Teaching and at the same time continues with EFL classes to keep her roots in classroom teaching. She is an examiner for various teacher education schemes in TEFL/TESL for the Royal Society of Arts and, as a teacher trainer, has worked on short courses around the world for The British Council. She is the author of *Pen to Paper, In a Word, In the Picture, Freestyle,* and *Using Readers in Language Teaching.*

Alan Maley worked for The British Council from 1962–1988, serving as English Language Officer in Yugoslavia, Ghana, Italy, France, and China, and as Regional Representative for The British Council in South India (Madras). He is currently Director-General of the Bell Educational Trust, Cambridge.

He wrote *Quartet* (with Françoise Greilet and Wim Welsing, OUP 1982). He has also written *Beyond Words, Sounds Interesting, Sounds Intriguing, Words, Variations on a Theme,* and *Drama Techniques in Language Learning* (all with Alan Duff), *The Mind's Eye* (with Françoise Grellet and Alan Duff), and *Learning to Listen* and *Poem into Poem* (with Sandra Moulding). He is also Series Editor for the Oxford Supplementary Skills Series.

Foreword

The teaching of writing to EFL/ESL students has tended to be sidelined in the scramble for communicative competence. Much current practice is still characterized by the construction of isolated sentences to reinforce the teaching of grammatical structures, by the use of models for controlled parallel production, or by a hope-for-the-best 'write an essay on X' approach.

Meantime, work in teaching the mother tongue both in the UK and the USA has been moving towards a process approach to writing. Rather than analysing the features of finished texts and attempting to teach students to reproduce them, this approach starts from an examination of what good writers actually *do as they write*. Processes such as jotting down ideas at random, organizing them, writing first drafts, and revising can then be made available to students.

In *Writing*, Tricia Hedge reflects this change of viewpoint, and attempts to apply its insights to the EFL/ESL context.

The emphasis throughout is on the process involved in producing complete, contextualized pieces of writing. She focuses especially on *why* the writing is being done (a sense of purpose) and *who* it is being written for (a sense of audience). The activities she offers are both highly practical, based as they are on her long and varied experience, and interesting to do. This is not to suggest that the nuts and bolts of grammatical and discoursal accuracy are neglected.

In the section *Crafting* she provides a rich array of more familiar tasks to complement the earlier process-orientated materials.

Teachers faced with the daunting task of marking pieces of written work will find her ideas on the process of marking refreshingly practical. Indeed, this is the most comprehensive and sensitive treatment of the subject I have yet seen.

There is a shortage of resource material which reflects current thinking in the area of writing. This book will go a long way to filling the gap.

Alan Maley

Introduction

Writers and writing

When I told my class of advanced students about an article I had been reading called 'Anguish as a Second Language' (Raimes 1983), which dealt with the problems of writing in a second language, they smiled at the pun but agreed with the sentiment. I think many students and teachers would recognize, if ruefully, the characterization of writing periods as times of sighing, pencil-chewing, foot-shuffling agony. Why is it that for large numbers of English language students writing seems to pose great problems? Possibly for the same reasons that large numbers of adult native speakers never achieve a high level of expressiveness in writing their first language. It is partly to do with the nature of writing itself. Harold Rosen (1981), writing about a schools curriculum project on writing in Britain, explained it in this way:

> The writer is a lonely figure cut off from the stimulus and corrective of listeners. He must be a predictor of reactions and act on his predictions. He writes with one hand tied behind his back, being robbed of gesture. He is robbed too of the tone of his voice and the aid of clues the environment provides. He is condemned to monologue; there is no one to help out, to fill the silences, put words in his mouth, or make encouraging noises.

As Rosen points out, writing is detached from the wide range of expressive possibilities in speech. A writer is unable to exploit all the devices available to a speaker: gesture, body movement, facial expression, pitch and tone of voice, stress, and hesitations. A speaker can backtrack, or clarify and revise ideas as listeners question or disagree. A writer has to compensate for all of these disadvantages.

Compared with speech, effective writing requires a number of things: a high degree of organization in the development of ideas and information; a high degree of accuracy so that there is no ambiguity of meaning; the use of complex grammatical devices for focus and emphasis; and a careful choice of vocabulary, grammatical patterns, and sentence structures to create a style which is appropriate to the subject matter and the eventual readers.

It is these demands which present particular problems to foreign writers of English. Even those who are proficient writers in their first language have to acquire a wide language base from which to make these choices. They may also find that confusing differences exist between the conventions of writing in their first language and English. For example, the level of formality or patterns of presenting information in letters may differ, or the accepted method of setting out arguments in discursive writing may vary.

The purpose of this resource book is to look at writers and writing in the English language classroom and to offer suggestions for helping students to overcome the difficulties they experience in developing clear, effective writing in English.

In general terms the resources are presented for teachers of teenage or adult learners of English as a second or foreign language, in that the content of the tasks is conceptually appropriate to these age groups. However, many of the principles at work in the tasks are equally applicable to the writing development of younger learners and the techniques could be incorporated into writing activities with content suitable for younger age groups.

I should also point out that the resources are primarily intended for teachers of general-purpose classes. The tasks have been used in and are adaptable to a variety of contexts, for example, the multilingual group of EFL short-course students, the ESL group of ethnic minority students, and the monolingual EFL class overseas. Some of the tasks have been derived from teaching college students who need to write English for academic purposes. However, more specialized forms of writing, such as extended academic essays or reports or commercial correspondence are not dealt with, as these require more consideration than a general resource book can usefully provide.

Establishing a framework for writing tasks

Writing has been a neglected area of English language teaching for some years. One only has to look at the large numbers of books available to the ELT profession on reading, and the scarcity of books on writing to see the imbalance. To take the comparison further, teachers have for some time been offered models of reading, principles for designing reading tasks, and practical suggestions for classroom methodology.

It is only recently, however, that research into writing has offered thought-provoking ideas about what good writers do, ideas which hold implications for teachers who wish to help their students to become good writers. In the absence of a well established or widely recognized model of writing, teachers tend to have very varying ideas about the role of writing in the classroom, what writing involves, and the possible roles of teachers and students in developing writing activities.

The approaches and activities presented in this book are based on a number of assumptions about writers and writing which I am going to set out in this introduction as a frame of reference for the resources presented later. Before reading through them, you may like to reflect on your own approach to writing, your own classroom practice and the assumptions it is based on. Here are some questions to guide your introspections:

Your personal approach to writing: a questionnaire

1 To what extent do you think of writing as a skill in its own right which can be taught in the classroom through a range of tasks and activities?

2 Why do your students write in their English classes? Make a list of all the reasons why you think that writing is important in English lessons.

3 Do your students have to pass examinations in English? What kinds of writing are required by the examinations?

4 What kinds of 'texts' do students write in your lessons? Make a list of typical writing tasks. How much time do they spend on:
   a. writing sentences?
   b. writing whole 'texts', e.g. narratives, descriptions, etc.?

5 To what extent do you think difficulty in foreign language writing is a language problem or a writing problem?

6 Can you introspect on your own writing in a first or foreign language? What are the difficulties you experience?

7 Do you work with your students when they are writing, encouraging them to revise and edit their work as they go along?

8 Do your students ever collaborate on writing tasks?

9 Do your students ever mark their own or each other's work?

10 Does writing take place in separate lessons in your students' programme or is it integrated with other work?

The questionnaire points to some of the currently debated issues in relation to the teaching of writing and its role in the learning of English. Many of these issues are discussed in the five sections of the book, each of which provides a framework and rationale for the resources. The questionnaire also suggests possibilities for classroom practice which are developed in the sets of tasks.

The assumptions made about writing in this resource book can be listed and elaborated in the following way:

1 The reasons for writing

A good deal of writing in the English language classroom is undertaken as an aid to learning, for example, to consolidate the learning of new structures or vocabulary or to help students remember new items of language. In this context, the role of writing is little different from its role in any other subject; it allows students to see how they are progressing and to get feedback from the teacher, and it allows teachers to monitor and diagnose problems. Much of this writing is at the sentence level and is what Ron White (1980) calls 'sentence level reinforcement exercises'.

They clearly have their value in language learning, but successful writing depends on more than the ability to produce clear and correct sentences. I am interested in tasks which help students to write whole pieces of communication, to link and develop information, ideas, or arguments for a particular reader or group of readers.

Writing tasks which have whole texts as their outcome relate appropriately to the ultimate goal of those learners who need to write English in their social, educational, or professional lives. Some of our students know already what they need to be able to write in English. Others may be uncertain about the nature of their future needs. Our role as teachers is to build communicative potential. Many secondary students have to prove their competence in English and sometimes in other subjects by producing compositions for examinations. In my own experience there have been substantial numbers of students who have no identifiable needs, present or future, for written English, but who enjoy writing, who are motivated to use their language resources in producing stories, reviews, essays, and even poems, simply to practise and improve their English. By encouraging the production of whole texts in the classroom, we can provide for these different motivations for writing.

Assumption 1
Classroom writing tasks should reflect the ultimate goal of enabling students to write whole texts which form connected, contextualized, and appropriate pieces of communication.

2 The product of writing

One approach to writing is to look at instances of writing and to analyse the features of written texts. This will tell us something about what it is that students have to produce. It is possible to build up a list of the 'skills' that writers need. It would include:
- getting the grammar right
- having a range of vocabulary
- punctuating meaningfully
- using the conventions of layout correctly, e.g. in letters
- spelling accurately
- using a range of sentence structures
- linking ideas and information across sentences to develop a topic
- developing and organizing the content clearly and convincingly.

It is also possible to build up a checklist of the forms (letters, essays, reports) and the functions (narrative, description, comparison, and contrast) of written texts and to show students how the features and organization of these different written products differ from one another. In setting and marking work teachers and students can focus on one or on a number of the general skills, but ideally within the context of a whole text.

Assumption 2
Students need opportunities to practise various forms and functions in writing and within these to develop the different skills involved in producing written texts.

3 The process of composing

Perhaps the most important insight that recent research into writing has given us is that good writers appear to go through certain processes which lead to successful pieces of written work. They start off with an overall plan in their heads. They think about what they want to say and who they are writing for. They then draft out sections of the writing and as they work on them they are constantly reviewing, revising, and editing their work. In other words, we can characterize good writers as people who have a sense of purpose, a sense of audience, and a sense of direction in their writing. Unskilled writers tend to be much more haphazard and much less confident in their approach.

Assumption 3
Classroom writing tasks need to be set up in ways that reflect the writing process in good writers. We need to encourage our students to go through a process of planning, organizing, composing, and revising.

4 The process of communicating

The process of writing involves composing, as suggested in point 3. It also involves communicating. Most of the writing we do in real life is written with a reader in mind – a friend, a relative, a colleague, an institution, or a particular teacher. Knowing who the reader is provides the writer with a context without which it is difficult to know exactly what or how to write. And yet it is possible to find writing tasks in some teaching materials which do not specify a context to help the student.

For example, a book I saw recently gave students a choice of compositions for homework, one of which was:

'Describe a place you know well.'

If I were a student I would want to know why and who for? Does the task require the kind of description we would find in a travel brochure, a visitor's guide, or a geography textbook? Or could I write about my home town in the way I would describe it to a pen-friend who has never visited it? Without a context it is difficult to know what to put in and what to leave out, or how formal or informal to be.

In other words, the selection of appropriate content and style depends on a sense of audience. One of the teacher's tasks is to create contexts and provide audiences for writing. Sometimes it is possible to write for real audiences, for example, a letter requesting information from an organization. Sometimes the teacher can create audiences by setting up 'roles' in the classroom for tasks in which students write to each other.

Assumption 4

When setting writing tasks, teachers need to vary the audience, identify who the readers are to be, and try to make every piece of writing fulfil some kind of communicative purpose, either real or simulated. When students understand the context they are much more likely to write effectively.

5 The process of improving

Helping our students with planning and drafting is only half of the teacher's task. The other half concerns our response to writing, a response which is important for a number of reasons:

a. writing requires a lot of conscious effort from students, so they understandably expect feedback and can become discouraged if it is not forthcoming.

b. learners monitor their writing to a much greater extent than they monitor their speech because writing is a more conscious process. It is probably true, then, that writing is a truer indication of how a student is progressing in the language and it can therefore give the teacher an opportunity for assessment and diagnosis of problem areas.

c. writing is much easier to revise than speech because it is permanent and therefore available. It is therefore possible for teachers to exploit writing for learning in several effective ways.

Responding positively to the strengths in a student's writing is important in building up confidence in the writing process. Ideally, when marking any piece of work, ticks in the margin and commendations in the comments should provide a counterbalance to correction of 'errors' in the script.

Even more important are moves to involve students in the revising and editing of their own work so that the activity known as 'marking' becomes part of the writing process and a genuine source of learning for both students and teachers. In other words, it becomes a process of *improving*.

Assumption 5

The process of marking, with its traditional focus on error-correction by the teacher needs review and modification into a range of activities involving students as well as teachers, thus making revision an integral part of the process of writing.

6 Time for writing

There is a widely held belief that in order to be a good writer a student needs to read a lot. This makes sense. It benefits students to be exposed to models of different text types so that they can develop awareness of what constitutes good writing. I would agree that reading is necessary and valuable but it is not sufficient. My own experience tells me that in order to become a good writer a student needs to write a lot. This is especially true of poor writers who tend to get trapped in a downward spiral of failure; they feel that they are poor writers, so they are not motivated to write and, because they seldom practise, they remain poor writers.

This situation is exacerbated in many classrooms where writing is mainly relegated to a homework activity. It is perhaps not surprising that writing often tends to be an out-of-class activity: many teachers feel that class time, often scarce, is best devoted to aural/oral work and homework to writing, which can then be done at the students' own pace.

However, many students would benefit from classroom practice in writing for which the teacher can prepare tasks with carefully worked out stages of planning, drafting, and revision. If poorer writers feel some measure of success in the supportive learning environment of the classroom, they will begin to develop the confidence they need to write more at home and so start on the upward spiral of motivation and improvement.

Assumption 6
Students need time in the classroom for writing. The teacher's task is to select or design activities which support them through the process of producing a piece of writing.

7 Working together on writing

Another very good reason for spending classroom time on writing is that it allows students to work together on writing in different ways. Although the teacher's ultimate aim is to develop the writing skills of each student individually, individual students have a good deal to gain from collaborative writing.

Group composition is a good example of an activity in which the classroom becomes a writing workshop, as students are asked to work together in small groups on a writing task. At each stage of the activity the group interaction contributes in useful ways to the writing process, for example:

a. brainstorming a topic in group discussion produces lots of ideas from which students have to select the most effective and appropriate. Careful selection of content is an important part of the art of good writing.

   b. skills of organization and logical sequencing come into play as
      the group decides on the overall structure of the piece of
      writing.
   c. while writing out a first draft, with one student acting as 'scribe'
      or secretary, and the other students arguing out the structures of
      sentences, the choice of words, and the best way to link ideas,
      there is a spontaneous process of revision in progress.

Group composition has the added advantage of enabling students to
learn from each other's strengths. It is an activity where stronger
students can help the weaker ones in the group. It also enables the
teacher to move around from group to group monitoring the work
and helping with the process of composition.

Assumption 7
Collaborative writing in the classroom generates discussions and
activities which encourage an effective process of writing.

All of the preceding seven assumptions underly the writing tasks
presented in the rest of the book. In setting them out here I have
raised a number of points which will be taken up and further
explored and exemplified in the relevant sections. But before
moving on, here is an immediate example of a task for elementary
students which will serve to illustrate some of the principles in
practice.

Describing a person
1 Ask students to work individually and to think of someone they
know and like, such as someone in their class, a girlfriend/
boyfriend, relative, etc. Ask them to write down five sentences. Use
prompt questions orally or on the blackboard to get them started.
– *Is he tall/thin?*
– *What colour is her hair?*

Dynamics
a. Students compose a first draft from their existing language
resources and personal experience. They are given a chance to
'create' before seeing a model.

b. A set of sentences comprise a first draft which can later be
revised and refined.

---

2 Then read a text which is a simple description of a person.
Provide a context for the text, for example, Barbara's description of
her new boyfriend in a letter to a friend:

He's quite tall and slim with fair curly hair and blue eyes.
He usually wears casual clothes. He likes wearing jeans
and a leather jacket. He's a lively person, very funny
sometimes but he can be serious too. Everyone likes
him because he's very kind.

Dynamics
a. Students are presented with a particular function of writing, e.g. physical description, and one possible organization for it.

b. Setting the context of an informal letter to a friend indicates to students that it is appropriate to write informally with contracted forms.

3 Work with the whole class together, eliciting words from the text and writing them down in three categories on the blackboard.

Looks	Clothes	Personality

Dynamics
Focus on a particular writing skill, i.e. choice of lexis to fit relevant categories.

4 Put students into groups of four and ask them to read out in turn the sentences they wrote in step 1, the whole group noting down new words in their lists. Monitor and help the groups.

Dynamics
Students interact to generate the thinking process and build up ideas for content.

5 You can then elicit new words from the groups and add to the lists on the blackboard (with any necessary spelling corrections and explanations).

6 Give each group a picture of a person (magazine cut-outs) and ask them to make notes together on the three categories.

Dynamics
Students are encouraged to make notes as a planning activity.

7 Take up some of the notes (jotted down while monitoring) and work on a sentence-level exercise practising the sentence structures in the model text, using adjectival phrases:
– *She's quite short and slim with dark, wavy hair, and brown eyes.*

Dynamics
Focus is on a particular writing skill, that is, specific types of sentence structure, but in the context of a whole text.

8 Ask the students to write a description of the person in their picture (in the group or in pairs) using the notes they have made, knowing that their classmates are going to use it for a matching game.

Dynamics

Collaborative writing ensures a process of revising and editing.

---

9 Display the completed pieces of writing on the classroom wall with the pictures as a matching game 'Who's who?'

Dynamics

The game creates an audience which will judge the effectiveness of the communication.

---

10 Ask the students to think back to the person they first tried to describe, and develop their original draft into a fuller description.

Dynamics

a. Students rethink, revise, and edit their first draft to produce a final draft.

b. Time has been provided for writing in the classroom. The homework allows students to try a similar task by themselves after a degree of confidence has been established.

How to use this book

How the book is organized

This book has been structured to reflect the stages of the writing process itself.

1 Composing
This section discusses the pre-writing and drafting stages when writers get their ideas together, make rough plans or formulate mental outlines, and develop a sense of direction as they begin to draft their writing. The tasks present a range of techniques for encouraging good pre-writing and drafting strategies in the process of composition.

2 Communicating
The focus is on one aspect of composing, the need to develop a strong sense of audience. The tasks demonstrate ways in which the teacher can create contexts for classroom writing and provide a range of readers.

3 Crafting
Here we look at the skills a writer needs to produce coherent and appropriate texts. The tasks suggest ways in which teachers can help learners to develop paragraphs coherently, to use cohesive devices, to use a range of sentence structures, and to develop a range of appropriate vocabulary.

4 Improving
Discussion centres on the ways in which teachers and learners can work together to improve the clarity and quality of writing. It includes ideas for involving students in the activities of redrafting and editing their work. It also investigates possible marking strategies for teachers and the development of marking policies within institutions.

5 Evaluating
This section considers criteria which teachers might apply in selecting or designing appropriate writing tasks and materials for their own learners.

The outcome of this type of organization is that there is a discrete focus in the tasks of each section on the topic of that section. For example, in *Composing* there is a task which demonstrates in detail the strategy of brainstorming. Brainstorming may then be mentioned in tasks in *Crafting* but will not be repeatedly described in detail. Similarly, *Improving* describes strategies such as group writing or pair-work editing which can be applied to any of the writing tasks described in the book. In this way it is possible to highlight each stage in the writing process and present a range of strategies without undue repetition.

A resource book is not meant to be a straight read, rather something to be dipped into. However, given the underlying rationale for the organization of the book, it would be useful to you as the reader, to skim through the various sections and gain an overall impression so that you can combine and integrate the resources.

I hope that you will be able to explore several possibilities in exploiting this set of resources.

– In some of the tasks, for example, 'A scene as a moment in time', it is possible to predict the language that learners will need – in this case, verbs of movement, the present progressive, and vocabulary items to describe the particular scene. Such tasks can be selected and adapted to form the end point in an integrated skills approach to the teaching of certain language items.
– Many of the tasks can be used as more open-ended fluency activities, giving learners the opportunity to use all the language resources they have acquired, after preliminary discussion of ideas and content, and with no particular focus on specific language items.
– If the strategies presented in *Improving*, such as conferencing and group writing are applied, then students become involved in accuracy work which is comparatively spontaneous and certainly more meaningful and motivating than highly-controlled writing exercises of a more traditional type.

In that the tasks present a range of techniques and strategies which can be applied in a variety of ways, they are not sequenced. As you browse through the book you will find a variety of ideas and can select according to your teaching situation and the particular needs of your learners. Each task is assigned to a level but, as you try out the suggestions, you will be able to adapt. Each task demonstrates a technique for encouraging good writing processes and may be adapted to a range of levels. The particular example chosen to illustrate the technique has a content which is appropriate to the given level, but I hope that you will be able to develop content suitable for your own types, ages, and levels of students.

How each activity is organized

The organization of each task in this resource book follows a similar format. You will find some or all of the following headings used to give the information relevant to the particular focus of each task. For example, in *Improving*, activities are presented which can be applied to any writing task. They are therefore described only in terms of the *level* or range of levels at which the technique may be introduced, the *preparation* needed, and the procedure to go through *in class*. Other sections may present more extended descriptions of tasks, and notes are given detailing the *topic*, *function*, *form*, *focus*, and *context* of the writing.

Level
Generally an indication of the minimum level at which the task can be successfully attempted by students. Sometimes the language required by a certain task can be adapted upwards or downwards to suit a particular group of your students and, in this case, a range of levels is given. In other cases, as mentioned earlier, I hope you will be able to take an idea and find suitable content for other levels of learners.

Topic
This refers to the content of the task. Sometimes the topic is not given, as the activity is more of a technique which can be generalized to many of the tasks in the book. Always check the task because you may often find that the content is flexible and you can transfer the ideas very quickly to another content area.

Function
Relates to the type of discourse organization required by the piece of writing, e.g. narrative, description, instruction, argument, comparison, etc.

Form
This is the form within which any of the discourse types listed above can be presented, e.g. a letter, a report, a guidebook, an information leaflet, or an academic essay.

Focus
Explains the writing skill or skills which the task aims to develop, such as paragraphing, selecting relevant content, using effective cohesive devices, etc.

Context
Refers to the real or projected reader or readers of the writing. For example, the following contexts for writing might be given to or created for students:
– You are writing a guide for visitors to your institution.
– You are practising a composition of the type you will need to write in your end-of-year examinations. It should be formal and academic.

Preparation
Anything you need to do or think about before you go into the classroom.

In class
A step-by-step procedure for carrying out the task in class.

Remarks
These may be introductory, immediately after the title, in which case they describe aims or relate the task to others in the section.

The remarks given at the end of activities may give warnings abou classroom exploitation, compare possible advantages and disadvantages of the task, suggest useful sources of further ideas, cross-refer to other sections of the book.

Variations
Some activities have variations that can be used with different type of classes at different levels.

1 Composing

Introduction

What exactly do we do as writers when we compose a piece of writing? What kind of behaviour, what stages, what activities do writers become involved in before and during writing? How do they get going, how do they keep going and what causes the 'blocks' that most of us have experienced at times when trying to write? What does the act of writing involve?

These are some of the questions which researchers into writing in a first and in a second language have addressed in the last decade. There is concensus among them on one essential feature – that writing is a *process*. In fact, it is a complex process with a number of operations going on simultaneously. Moreover, some writers seem to have a much better understanding of how to make the process work effectively for them and consequently produce more successful pieces of writing.

These findings hold significant implications for the classroom. Can teachers help students, to a much greater extent than is current practice, with the process of composition? In many English language classrooms the pattern has been to set written work, perhaps with some discussion beforehand, and then to mark the incoming pieces of writing. In other words, the traditional focus has been much more on the end result of the composition process, that is, the *product* of writing. Research now seems to suggest that we could be as much concerned with responding to the student *writer* as to the student's *writing*.

It would certainly be useful for us as teachers to investigate the process of composition and to find out what it entails so that we can reflect on the problems it may present to our students. Then we will be in a better position to develop the most effective and helpful classroom practice.

As writers ourselves and as classroom teachers we can begin our investigations through introspection and observation. For example, think about the following:

1 Reflect on the process you go through when you
a. write a letter to a friend
b. write a report for your colleagues.

How do you start in each case? Do you think for a period before you write? Do you make a plan? Is your planning accompanied by note-making?

Note down the various strategies you use while you are writing. Do you stop and read through what you have written? How often do you read from the beginning again? How many times do you cross out or go back and put in extra sentences?

2 Observe a class of students writing. See what differences exist in their writing behaviour.

3 Talk to your students about how they write, what problems they have, and how they feel about writing.

One of the things I have done in recent years is to find out how my intermediate students perceive the process of writing and to match their introspections about how they write with what they write. With a new group it is useful to set a short writing task and ask the students as they write to introspect on the strategies they are using and to make some jottings. Here are some extracts which show the different approaches that learners took when asked to write about someone they admired.

- First I made a list of words in my notebook.
- I thought of a sentence to write down. Then I thought of some more and added them.
- I wrote down some sentences in my book. Then I crossed them out and started again.
- I wrote a page very quickly. Then I went from the beginning. I turned round some sentences to make a new organization.
- I wrote: 'The person I most admire is . . .'. Then I stopped and thought for a few minutes. I wrote some notes in the margin: 'Close friend', 'Chilean refugee'. Then I wrote the end of the sentence. I added some more ideas quickly.

These notes gave me insights into the different strategies writers adopt and into the problems that some of the poorer writers experience.

This simple investigation into my own students' writing is a crude imitation of the careful and detailed studies made over the last decade. A major focus of those studies has been on what skilled writers do, as opposed to unskilled writers. Let us look at some of the information and insights which such studies have made available to teachers and then go on to consider the implications for classroom practice.

What do we know about the process of writing?

In brief, the process of writing contains a number of stages which can be represented in the following figure:

being
motivated ——→ getting ——→ planning ——→ making ——→ making ——→ revising ——→ editing and
to   ideas   and   notes   a first   replanning   getting
write   together   outlining   draft   redrafting   ready for
                                                                                                        publication

Figure 1

However, the figure oversimplifies matters because, although writing in general involves these overall stages, the process of composition is not a linear one, moving from planning to composing to revising and to editing. It would be more accurate to characterize writing as a recursive activity in which the writer moves backwards and forwards between drafting and revising, with stages of replanning in between. As Shaughnessy (1977) describes it, it is 'a messy process that leads to clarity'.

Frank Smith (1982) represents this messy process in terms of the ways in which the text is moved around, modified, cut, or expanded:

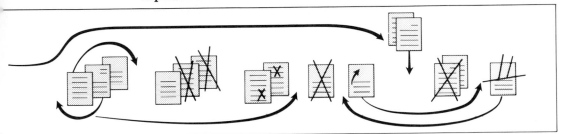

Figure 2

It is also important to point out that the amount of time spent on any part of the process will depend on the type of writing. For example, in writing a letter to a friend with the purpose of bringing her up to date with family news, one may well scribble down a list of things to include, but the planning is not likely to be as elaborate as when writing a report for colleagues at work on a matter of serious concern.

The process of writing is often described as consisting of three major activities or groups of activities:

1 Pre-writing

Before putting pen to paper, the skilled writer in real life considers two important questions:

a. **What is the purpose of this piece of writing?** This first question is to do with *function*. For example, is it a report which the writer hopes will be persuasive and stimulate action? Is it an explanation of how something works, which has to be careful, detailed, and clear? Is it a letter of invitation to some friends or a letter applying for a job? The purpose of the writing will influence the choice of organization and the choice of language. (This aspect of writing is considered in more detail in the section called *Crafting*.)

b. Who am I writing this for? The second question is to do with *audience*. The reader may be an individual, one you know well, or a group of colleagues, an institution, an examiner, or a tutor. Thinking about the eventual reader(s) helps the writer to select what to say and how to present it in the most appropriate style – formal, friendly, serious, or tentative. (This aspect of writing is taken up in detail in the next section, *Communicating*.)

The answers to these two questions provide the writer with a sense of purpose and a sense of audience, in other words, a writing context which significantly influences the first stage of the composition process, that of exploring possible content and planning outlines.

The good writer generates plans for writing at this stage though, as we have seen, the amount of planning varies. We could draw a scale from comparatively spontaneous writing to very carefully planned writing and place different kinds of writing on it in appropriate places.

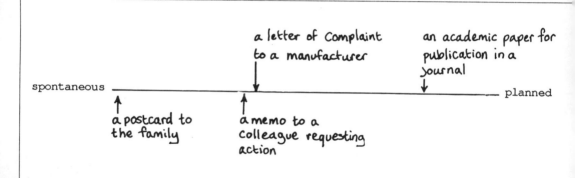

Figure 3

So, planning as a process may involve a variety of things: a set of five points jotted down to include in a letter home; more detailed notes and an outline plan; or a mental outline such as: 'I'll start by describing the problems, then I'll suggest two alternatives; I'll give the Nigerian example and discuss its advantages, then . . .'.

However, even when quite elaborate outlines are prepared, good writers change their ideas as they write and reshape their plans. Widdowson (1983) points to this tendency:

In writing one so frequently arrives at a destination not originally envisaged, by a route not yet planned for in the original itinerary.

In fact, it is the poorer writers who see plans as strait-jackets and who follow the original plan through rigorously without deviation and without allowing the interplay between writing and thinking that can create new ideas and lead to improvements.

2 Writing and rewriting

The second phase of activity is the writing itself and with good writers this consists of making a first draft. But writing the first draft is often interrupted as the writer stops to read over and review, to get an idea of how the text is developing, to revise plans, and bring in new ideas or rearrange those already expressed. There is a good deal of recycling in the process from planning to drafting, reviewing, replanning, revising, etc. Good writers tend to concentrate on getting the content right first and leave details like correcting spelling, punctuation, and grammar until later.

Revision involves assessing what has already been written and deciding on points like these:

– Am I sharing my impressions clearly enough with my reader?
– Have I missed out any important points of information?
– Are there any points in the writing where my reader has to make a 'jump' because I've omitted a line of argument or I've forgotten to explain something?
– Does the vocabulary need to be made stronger at any point?
– Are there some sentences which don't say much or which are too repetitive and can be missed out?
– Can I rearrange any sets of sentences to make the writing clearer or more interesting?
– Do I need to rearrange any paragraphs?
– Are the links between sections clear? Do they guide my reader through the writing?

In summary, the drafting process focuses primarily on *what* the writer wants to say, while redrafting progressively focuses on *how* to say it most effectively.

3 Editing

The post-writing stage consists of reading through and trying to apply a reader's perspective in order to assess how clearly readers might follow the ideas. The editing process makes the final readjustments and checks accuracy so that the text is maximally accessible to the reader. Some poorer writers tend not to engage in editing but assume that their writing is clear to others because it is clear to them. Alternatively, poor writers may concentrate throughout the whole writing process on accuracy in grammar, punctuation, etc., without considering whether or not the overall structure is clear. They continually move from drafting to editing without any in-between stages of rethinking and reorganization. It is a less-than-effective process that might well be unwittingly encouraged by teachers whose strategy for marking is to correct only minor problems on the surface of the writing without commenting on any major problems in structure. This is an understandable strategy on the part of teachers, given the amount of marking most of us have to do. The problem and possible solutions are discussed in *Improving*.

What are the implications of this knowledge for the classroom?

The first question we perhaps need to ask as teachers is whether or not adult foreign language learners need to be 'taught' the process of successful composition or if in any way they need help in developing good strategies for writing. Can we not assume that writing skills learned in a first language will transfer successfully to a second language?

Experience suggests that it would be unwise to assume that all students, or even the majority of students, are skilled writers in their mother tongue. Large numbers of young adults leave school without ever becoming proficient writers.

Clearly EFL writers need help with linguistic form, i.e. with grammar, sentence structure, and so on. They often need help with the organization of texts as well, since conventions for this can differ from one language to another. But there is also a strong argument for saying that teachers need to concern themselves and their English language students with the process of composition. Ann Raimes (1983) makes this point from her experience of working with adult ESL students:

> Students who do read and write well in the first language also need to work on the new creative activity of forming ideas in English for English-speaking audiences.

The next question, then, is in what ways teachers can develop classroom practices which will help students with the process of composition. Essentially, the teacher's role is to provide an environment in which students will learn about writing, see models of good writing, get plenty of practice in writing, and receive help during the writing process. The tasks in this resource book are based on the following principles:

1 Teenage and adult students are aware of their own problems in writing, and they have attitudes and feelings about the writing process. Teachers can play a valuable part in raising awareness of the process of composition by talking explicitly about the stages of writing as well as by structuring tasks to take account of this.

2 Teachers can play a support role during the early stages of the composition process by helping students to get their ideas together. This can be done by talking about things to generate ideas, by doing things such as interviewing other students, by pooling information, ideas, or opinions in the class, by working from pictures, or by reading texts of various kinds.

3 The teacher can also provide good models for writing, indirectly, by encouraging good reading habits but also directly, when appropriate, by analysing textual structure, particularly with some types of more formal academic writing.

4 Planning activities structured by the teacher can help students to develop a sense of direction in their writing, though they should always be encouraged to regard a plan as an enabling device or support rather than as a rigid control.

5 Teachers can encourage the drafting process by creating a workshop atmosphere in their classrooms, to the extent of providing rough paper, scissors, paste, erasers, etc. And, while monitoring writing in progress, they can suggest that these are used for chopping and changing the structure of the text. Teachers can support the drafting process in various ways. They can intervene quietly, questioning and advising, in order to help writers get their ideas down on paper in English. Or they can encourage students to read each other's work and suggest restructurings and revisions. Giving help during writing proves far more effective than giving it afterwards.

The advent of the word processor in institutions which can afford the technology has great potential for encouraging students to develop revision strategies. Rewriting is more motivating when it can be done quickly, easily, and relatively painlessly by moving pieces of the text around. Alternatives can be evaluated and improvements immediately appreciated on the display screen.

6 Students need opportunities to engage in writing as a holistic process of composition. This means that they need practice in writing whole pieces of communication, not just controlled exercises in sentence structure, grammar, or bits and pieces of paragraph development. These activities have their place, as students need to be accurate in their writing, but they are not sufficient in themselves.

Brumfit (1984) comments on the need for writers to be able to produce English 'without so many errors that it would be demotivating to the writer' but at the same time he points out the problem of highly controlled writing exercises, in that they offer writing 'solely as a semi-conscious operation with no construction of meaning . . . only of form'.

One answer is to work with individual students on correcting errors in their own drafts so that the focus on accuracy takes place within the context of work already produced. Another is to offer a series of writing tasks which focus on aspects of accuracy but which take place within the context of whole texts. (This approach can be seen in many of the tasks in *Crafting*.)

In summary, the classroom needs to provide an environment in which students can experience being writers, thinking about purpose and audience, drafting a piece of writing, revising it, and sharing it with others.

The tasks on the following pages contain ideas and techniques for the pre-writing stages. Activities for rewriting and editing can be found in the section *Improving*, which investigates ways in which students and teachers can work together to monitor and improve writing. Many of the tasks demonstrate basic techniques for encouraging thinking, getting ideas together, outlining, and planning. They can be used for a wide range of topics and text types. All of them attempt to encourage an effective process of composition.

1.1 Gathering information

In the 'getting ready to write' stage, students seem to have several problems with motivation to write, thinking what to say, and organizing ideas before writing. The topic and activities in this task are designed to help teenagers and younger learners 'get ready' for writing. The task places emphasis on careful preparation, when students can think out and talk out ideas and explore possibilities. If students learn to organize information and ideas in expressive writing which is primarily for themselves, it should help them with the same process in other kinds of writing.

LEVEL

Lower intermediate (suitable for teenagers and younger learners)

TOPIC

My earliest years

PREPARATION

You can do this activity simply with blackboard and chalk and with students using their notebooks. However, it makes it more attractive if you:

a. Make a family tree (like the one shown in Figure 4) as a wall chart.
b. Bring photographs of your own childhood or ask the students to bring some of their own from home.
c. Study the questionnaire overleaf.
d. Make copies of suggestions for things to write about.

IN CLASS

1 Introduce the idea of an autobiography by asking students to say what their earliest memories are. You could preface this by describing your own earliest memory. It is best to give students a minute to tell each other their memories or to think individually for a moment before eliciting a few memories for the class to hear.

2 Emphasize that an autobiography is a *personal* history. Students choose exactly what *they* want to put in it. Give out the copies of 'Things to write about' and ask each student to tick the topics they have memories of and that they might like to write about, and suggest they add other topics.

Things to write about	Tick here (✓)
My family Where I was born My house My toys My relatives A special day The day we moved house The day I went to hospital	

NOTE: *You may make photocopies of this for classroom use (but please note that copyright law does not normally permit multiple copying of published material).*

3 Ask students to work in pairs and to show each other the photographs they have brought of things from their own childhood. They should try to describe the times, places, and events. At the end of this activity ask them to write down any new points in the list of 'Things to write about' which their conversations have suggested.

4 Elicit suggestions from the class as to how they can find out about their early childhood, and who they could ask. A way to start this is to show them the family tree and ask:

– *What is this?*
– *Can you make one for your family?*
– *Who can you ask to help you in your family?*
– *Are there any friends of the family you could ask?*

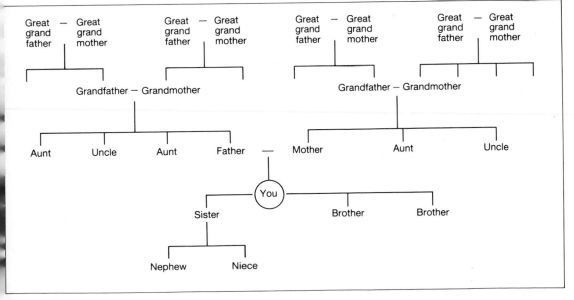

Figure 4

5 Then ask students to think carefully about what they can ask. Put them in groups to make a short questionnaire like the one shown below, filling in topics and people to ask.

What can you tell me about?	Grandparents	Parents	Aunts & uncles	Older brothers & sisters
My parents when I was very young My house My brothers and sisters My personality Special occasions I remember				

6 Conduct a feedback session in which a questionnaire combining ideas from different groups can be written up on the blackboard.

7 Students can then be asked to begin their 'research' for homework and to make notes from which to draft out the first chapter of their autobiography 'My earliest years'.

REMARKS

The steps outlined above are the initial steps in the classroom for a topic which could be extended into an autobiography with several chapters, depending on the interest generated. The next task in this section, in which the topic is 'First day at school', could be incorporated into another chapter of the autobiography.

The research carried out by the students at home will clearly have to be performed in their first language but this should not detract from the writing task itself.

1.2 Pyramid planning

LEVEL

Lower intermediate upwards

TOPIC

First day at school

PREPARATION

1 Copy the list opposite onto the blackboard or make copies for individual students.

2 You will need copies of 'First Day', from *Black Boy* by Richard Wright if you wish to integrate reading with writing. Otherwise you can give the story a dramatic reading while the students listen.

IN CLASS

1 You can use the story for initial motivation. It focuses on a particular experience and may trigger in the students specific memories which you can elicit and exploit.

2 Elicit from the class any specific memories of individuals' experiences of their first day at school. This could be primary, secondary, or high school.

3 Ask students to work individually for a couple of minutes to make a list of things which might be included in an account of a first day. You could initiate the list with some suggestions as shown below.

What you can remember about:
— how you went to school — what time school started and finished — your uniform (if you had one) — your classroom — your teacher — (other)

4 Divide the class into pairs and ask each pair to compare and discuss their points for a few moments.

5 Finally, organize the students into groups of four, each member from a different pair to ensure the widest possible exchange of ideas. Each student should then have a comprehensive list of points to think about as he/she starts drafting a personal experience of 'First day at school'.

TEXT

First Day

But I was still shy and half paralysed in the presence of a crowd and my first day at the new school made me a laughing stock of the classroom. I was sent to the blackboard to write my name and address. I knew my name and address, knew how to write it, how to spell it; but standing at the blackboard with the eyes of the many boys and girls on my back made me freeze inside and I was unable to write a single letter.

'Write your name,' the teacher called to me. I lifted the white chalk to the blackboard and, as I was about to write, my mind went blank; I could not remember my name, even the first letter. Somebody giggled and I stiffened.

'Just forget us and write your name and address,' the teacher called.

An impulse to write would flash through me, but my hand would refuse to move. The children began to titter and I flushed hotly.

'Don't you know your name?' the teacher asked.

I looked at her and could not answer. The teacher rose and walked to my side, smiling at me to give me confidence. She placed her hand tenderly upon my shoulder.

'What's your name?' she asked.

'Richard,' I whispered.

'Richard what?'

'Richard Wright.'

'Spell it.'

I spelled my name in a wild rush of letters, trying desperately to redeem my paralysing shyness.

'Spell it slowly so I can hear it,' she directed me.

I did.

'Now, can you write?'

'Yes, ma'am.'

'Then write it.'

Again I turned to the blackboard and lifted my hand to write, then I was blank and void within. I tried frantically to collect my senses but I could remember nothing. A sense of the boys and girls behind me filled me to the exclusion of everything. I realized how utterly I was failing and I grew weak and leaned my hot forehead against the cold blackboard. The room burst into a loud and prolonged laugh and my muscles froze. I sat and cursed myself. Why did I always appear so dumb when I was called upon to perform in a crowd? I knew how to write as well as any pupil in the classroom , and no doubt I could read better than any of them, and I could talk fluently and expressively when I was sure of myself. Then why did strange faces make me freeze? I sat with my ears and neck burning, hearing the pupils around me whisper, hating myself, hating them.

1.3 Making mind maps

Making a mind map is a strategy for note-making before writing; in other words, scribbling down ideas about the topic and developing those ideas as the mind makes associations. The topic used for demonstration below is the festival of Christmas, which would be appropriate to certain groups of students. However, the strategy can be used to explore almost any topic.

LEVEL	**Intermediate to advanced**
TOPIC	**A festival**
PREPARATION	This activity is best carried out quite simply with blackboard and chalk so that students grasp the idea of drawing a mind map as a spontaneous pre-writing activity.
IN CLASS	1 Ask students to close their eyes and think of Christmas. They should jot down all the things associated with Christmas that come into their minds. Set a definite time limit (one or two minutes). Let them jot down things in their first language if they do not know the English words. They can then start sharing what they have jotted down. As they listen to other students making suggestions and to your explanations and corrections, they will learn the English words for the ideas which they have tried to jot down. This is an invaluable way in which to learn vocabulary.
	2 Elicit ideas from the students as they suggest things, and make a collective mind map on the blackboard as the ideas are suggested, so that they can see how you draw out aspects of the topic and subgroup items. The reasoning behind mind maps is that we do not think in an ordered or linear way, but rather explore a topic by moving between its various aspects. The map may look something like this when it is under way, but elements would be added in random fashion:

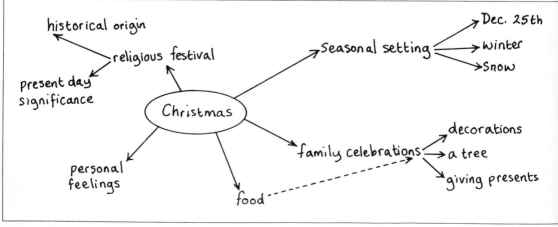

Figure 5

Branches can be drawn and added as students suggest new ideas or add ideas to already established aspects. The end result is a map with a number of subtopics or aspects radiating from the central topic and with further points added to these. Where there are links (Christmas food is, in one sense, an aspect of family celebrations), a line can be drawn associating them.

3 When the map is reasonably full, you can lead a class discussion on the best order in which points could be presented in a composition. In order to do this, it is necessary to provide a context and audience. For example, if describing Christmas in a letter to a friend overseas, the writer might begin with personal feelings or family celebrations. If writing a formal composition to the title 'Describe a festival in your own country', the writer might begin with the seasonal setting or the historical origin.

4 Alternative writing tasks are then possible:
a. You can set a writing task and encourage students to prepare a piece of writing using the mind map on the blackboard, elaborating it in their own way.
b. You could ask students to choose another festival and draw up personal mind maps for it.

5 Encourage the students to begin the process of composition and to show their work to classmates as they write, in order to get feedback and make appropriate revisions.

REMARKS

Once the idea of making mind maps has been established, students can be encouraged to use the strategy in subsequent writing tasks where note-making is appropriate as a pre-writing activity. The advantage of mind maps as an organizing strategy, particularly with descriptions, is that all the aspects of a topic are seen in relation and in proportion to each other, and possible links between paragraphs or sections of an essay become easily apparent.

1.4 Using a diagram of ideas

LEVEL

Intermediate to advanced

TOPIC

'Books, plays, and films should never be censored.'

PREPARATION

In this activity you should elicit ideas from the whole class. These can then be used by individual students for the content of their writing. Ideally your students will provide all the necessary content but it is as well to be prepared. For example, in the task below, the writing is a formal composition of the type popular in many educational systems or public examinations in English. It requires a discursive essay of the 'for and against' type. The title is:

'Books, plays, and films should never be censored.' Discuss the arguments for and against this assertion.

You would be well advised to prepare possible arguments before the lesson to prompt students or supplement those provided by the class.

IN CLASS

1 Introduce the title and ask students to think for a moment whether they agree or not with the statement and how they can justify their opinions.

2 Ask for one student to volunteer an argument for the statement and then for one to argue against it. Use these arguments to begin the diagram on the blackboard (see below for format).

3 Ask students to work in small groups. Each group should elaborate the points for and against. It is useful to set a time limit for this step, one appropriate to the level of the group.

4 Elicit arguments from the class to build up the diagram, but do not exhaust all the possibilities. Students should have ideas remaining to add to their own writing. During the process of eliciting arguments, you have an opportunity to provide vocabulary and useful structures.

5 Students can then begin the process of composition, using the ideas provided by the diagram and adding their own as their writing stimulates new ideas.

REMARKS

The technique outlined here is also suitable for the 'Discuss the advantages and disadvantages . . .' type of essay. Eliciting arguments from the class is particularly useful, as language can be provided by the teacher within the contexts that students find for themselves as they try to express ideas in English. A very good source of ideas for this activity is L.G. Alexander: *For and Against*.

Arguments for and against censorship

```
- censorship is necessary to
  protect children
- censorship is for the general
  good of society                    - people should be allowed to
- censors are liberal people and       hear, see, and read what they
  make sensible decisions              like
- unscrupulous people make money     - censorship is a denial of
  out of people's weaknesses           personal liberty
- pornography encourages             - censorship doesn't lead to
  immorality                           immorality but repression does
- violence in films brutalizes       - censorship does not prevent
  people                               pornography; the latter just
-                                      disappears into a 'black market'
-                                    - censors are poor discriminators
                                       of what is 'art': they often ban
                                       or cut works of artistic merit
                                     -
                                     -
      for
                                              against
```

1.5 Selecting and focusing information

Using a picture to plan a description is a useful technique for helping students to see the importance of logical development in description which is non-chronological. A writer has to decide how best to describe something so that the reader can reconstruct a true image of it. This means deciding what to focus on and how to relate the various elements.

LEVEL

Elementary to upper intermediate (depending on the picture chosen)

TOPIC

An interesting scene or still life

PREPARATION

You will need to make a collection of pictures, cut out magazine pictures or postcards, sufficient for a class set. If these are backed on card they will make a useful permanent resource. The pictures must be clear and show a number of objects or people in relationship to each other. Still life or scenes are most appropriate, as in the examples.

IN CLASS

1 Give each student a picture. Ask him/her to study it closely and look at each part of the picture in turn. Can they describe the scene as clearly in words as the photographer/artist has captured it?

2 As the students are looking at their pictures, ask them to decide which is the most important or most striking thing in the picture.

3 Ask students individually to write a first draft of a paragraph describing the picture.

4 As they finish working, write the following questions on the blackboard:
– *What is the focus of the picture and where is it in the picture?*
– *Where have you described the focus in your paragraph?*
– *Have you followed a certain order in your writing, e.g. foreground to background, right to left, according to the importance of the parts from your perspective?*
– *Could you improve on the order?*
– *How will your paragraph change if you move the order around?*

5 Encourage students to review their own work and to start redrafting.

1.6 Brainstorming

One of the most difficult tasks for many writers, especially when dealing with some of the more 'imaginative' topics set by teachers when preparing students for public examinations, is trying to think of things to write about. It is a classic stumbling block. Help is most usually provided by talking about the topic before writing begins. This can be undertaken in pairs or groups or with the whole class. Brainstorming is an activity which aims to help students with this important pre-writing stage of getting ideas together. In the task below it is a pair-work activity.

LEVEL

Elementary to advanced

TOPIC

A childhood memory

PREPARATION

If students are at an appropriate level, you can begin this activity with some short texts in which writers describe childhood memories. Good sources of these are Flora Thompson: *Larkrise to Candleford* or Helen Keller: *The Story of My Life*.
Alternatively, you may begin by telling students one of your own childhood memories.

IN CLASS

1 Either let students skim through the short texts you have selected or tell them about a memory of your own from your childhood, something vivid with clear sensations.

2 Ask if anyone in the class remembers something equally vivid and let them describe some of the sensations they remember.

3 Ask students to write down as many memories as they can and tell them not to worry about clarity or language as no one else will look at their notes. It is a good idea to suggest a five-minute time limit for this activity.

4 If students seem to have a block, suggest that they close their eyes and think of a scene from childhood, remembering the *sounds, sights, smells,* and *tastes* if suitable.

5 Ask students to work in pairs. They should discuss selected memories with their partners, talking about the ideas in their notes.

6 Then allow for another short period of note-making of any ideas or associations which the discussion generated.

7 Ask students to choose one of the memories they have jotted down and to consider the circumstances associated with it, i.e. the season, the time, the setting, the people around, the incident, and to write down notes on all of these.

8 Again, students should talk about the experience with their partners.

9 Students should now have plenty of ideas for writing a composition on 'A childhood memory', and can begin the process of writing.

REMARKS

I have used this technique with a group of sixteen upper intermediate students, selecting passages from Laurie Lee: *Cider with Rosie*, Elspeth Huxley: *The Flame Trees of Thika*, and James Joyce: *Portrait of the Artist as a Young Man*, all of which also helped to set the style the students could develop. The idea is based on a set of activities in Ron White's book, *Writing: Advanced*, in which he develops the topic of food and its associations.

1.7 Organizing points

The previous strategy of brainstorming is especially useful in creative writing where a spontaneous and unstructured flow of thoughts is a good way to get ideas together. Brainstorming can also be effective as the first stage in more formal types of writing, for example, for bringing to the surface of the mind all the information one knows about a certain topic. However, some forms of writing are probably best tackled with a more structured approach from the beginning. Structure is required before putting pen to paper; it also implies a process of controlling ideas. The following task aims to help students organize ideas to produce more formal pieces of writing.

LEVEL

Intermediate

TOPIC

My home country

PREPARATION

Choose a topic which involves a description and which lends itself to listing content and grouping it into sections. The topic chosen here is to describe a country. Students will be asked to write a formal composition on their own country. Prepare a list of points which you feel should be covered in this topic.

IN CLASS

1 Introduce the topic and ask students what items they think should go into a composition of this type. Write a list of suggestions on the blackboard as they are offered. Prompt students if they 'dry up' with items from the list you have prepared.

2 Give students your list of points and ask them to add any points from the blackboard which are not already listed.

3 Explain that some points in the list are headings and cover or subsume other points. Ask them to work out the headings and the points they cover.

4 When each student has finished this task, you can organize checking between partners.

5 Students decide next on the order of points. This can be done individually, in pairs, or as a whole class with you. If done in pairs or individually, there should be a feedback session to discuss the

criteria for organization (i.e. is there some kind of logical order, does one section naturally lead on to another, what is the best point at which to begin or to end?).

6 Students now have a list which they can use to organize their own pieces of writing. However, they should be encouraged to review the list and add items or categories which are particularly relevant to their own country.

Here is a list to demonstrate the task:

political parties	national examinations
colleges and universities	mountain regions
energy sources	sports
the delta area	agriculture
seasons	rainfall
national costume	exports
the assembly of representatives	festivals
economy	political system
typical foods	the people
power of the president	geography
the central river valley	manufacturing industry
education	elementary schools
tourism	

REMARKS

The major purpose of this task is to show students how planning for more formal pieces of writing can consist of three activities: listing, selecting and grouping, and organizing. As with other tasks, a balance between given material and the opportunity to add, develop, and create content is advisable, so that students learn to appreciate that plans should be used in a flexible way and are subject to revision.

1.8 Imagining dialogues

This is a particularly useful planning device for writing letters. The basic idea is that student writers imagine the conversation that might replace the letter. In other words they visualize their audience and work out the dialogue had the interaction been verbal rather than in letter form. In this way they can imagine the questions that the 'reader' might ask. It is a technique which ensures that all the relevant content is included and ordered in a sensible manner. It works well with formal letters, such as making requests, applications, etc.

LEVEL

Elementary to intermediate

TOPIC

A letter of application

PREPARATION

1 You will need a simple model letter of application which can be analysed in terms of implicit questions.

2 The lesson also requires a prompt for letter writing, one which is appropriate to the students. The advertisements in this task are one such prompt and would be appropriate to young European students who wish to spend a year in Britain after leaving school. Alternatively, students can prepare for the lesson by finding an advertisement for a job which they would like to do and are qualified for. If they are studying in England this will engage them in useful independent reading of newspapers and other materials. If the search is carried out in their first language, the letter itself can still be written in English and based on the job description.

IN CLASS

1 Give out copies of the letter below. Working with the whole class, ask them to imagine the conversation between this writer and the employer and to work out the question which might generate the first sentence as a response. Write the question on the blackboard.

2 Ask the students to work in pairs and to continue listing the questions which would generate the various parts of the letter.

26 Brookbank Road,
Chalkside,
Surrey SN5 3BQ
April 27th 1988

The Managing Director,
Sinton Exports Ltd,
3 Castle Chambers,
Chalkside,
Surrey.

Dear Sir,
I saw your advertisement for the post of bilingual secretary in the Gazette last Thursday. I would like to apply for the position. I am twenty-two years old, Italian, and speak German and English. My German is fluent as I lived in Germany for five years and attended High School there. After leaving school I returned to Italy and took a course of Secretarial Studies. I enclose a copy of my School Certificate and my Diploma in Secretarial Studies. I worked in Rome for six months as secretary to the manager of a small export company.
I came to England a year ago to improve my English and have taken the Cambridge Proficiency Examination in English and a course of English for Secretaries. I enclose copies of the certificates which I received for these.
I shall look forward to hearing from you.

Yours faithfully
Claudia Cremisi

3 Elicit the questions from the students and complete the list on the blackboard. It will probably look something like this:

- *Where did you see our advertisement?*
- *How old are you?*
- *What nationality are you?*
- *What languages do you speak?*
- *How good is your German?*
- *What secretarial qualifications do you have?*
- *Do you have certificates or diplomas for these?*
- *What work experience do you have?*
- *How long have you been in England?*
- *Have you taken any English language examinations?*

4 Give out copies of appropriate advertisements or ask the students to study their own advert. Each student should work out the set of questions which the employer might ask and write them out, deciding on a sensible order.

5 Students can then check each other's questions in pairs and suggest additions, deletions, or modifications.

6 Ask the students to start work on a first draft, following the set of questions.

REMARKS

This activity is also useful for redrafting in letter-writing. When students have written a first draft they can then work out the questions for their own or a partner's letter. This will help them to judge whether any content is absent, superfluous, or unclear.

SAMPLE ADVERTISEMENTS

The Grouse

Full and part-time positions available in this famous country inn for bar person and serving staff. Excellent working conditions and unusually good rates of pay to right applicants.

For further details please apply to:
**The Manager,
Aston Lea 950.**

General Clerical Staff

Young person required for busy solicitors' office. Work hours 8.30 - 5.00. Duties involve typing, telephone, reception and general office work. Salary according to age and experience. No knowledge of law required. Would suit person able to learn and work on own initiative.

Applications in writing to:
**Peter Bury, Spiller and Son,
14 Ship Street, Oxford.**

Full-Time Sales Assistants

Mayday Incorporated are looking for young and enthusiastic sales staff for our new showroom opening shortly in the West London area. We specialize in first and second world war memorabilia and other historical items.

Please write giving age, qualifications, and any experience to:
**Major Roderick Simpson,
Mayday Incorporated,
123 Baker Street,
London W1.**

1.9 Combining information

EVEL   **Intermediate to advanced**

OPIC   **An accident report**

PREPARATION   1 You need to find two articles from different newspapers
describing the same event. A good source of these is a range of city
or local papers, which tend to contain human interest stories like
the one shown in the task below. Try to ensure that the texts are
approximately the same length and will take the same amount of
time to read. You need enough copies of each for half the class.

2 Decide on a set of categories for note-making which suit the type
of text. For example, the texts below are reports of incidents. They
contain the essential elements of reports which lend themselves to
categories such as Who?, When?, What?, How?, etc.

N CLASS   1 Ask the whole class to imagine themselves as reporters about to
investigate a near-fatal accident. What would they want to find out
about it?

2 Elicit some categories of information from the class and write
them on the blackboard. Supplement them with your own
predetermined categories. Appropriate categories for the
newspaper articles below might be written as questions:

– *What sort of incident was it?*
– *Where did it take place?*
– *When did it happen?*
– *Who was involved?*
– *What happened to each of the people?*
– *What was the outcome?*
– *How did the people feel?*

3 Ask students to read their own articles and make notes, detailing
the information they can find for each category.

4 Put the students in pairs. Each pair should consist of a student
who has read article **A** and one who has read article **B**. Ask each
pair to compare notes and add any extra details their partner gives
them.

5 Ask students to write up their own articles from the notes they
have made and to make up their own headlines.

REMARKS   The advantage of this kind of task is that it provides students with
content and is thus complementary to tasks where students create
their own original texts. Eliciting categories helps students to see
the basic elements of this type of newspaper report and thereby to
appreciate one type of discourse structure. A possible disadvantage
is that students may be tempted to follow the language of the
original article too closely. In order to avoid this they should be
encouraged to work primarily from their notes. At the same time,

imitating or incorporating expressions from the model may be a useful language learning process as long as, on other occasions, students also have the chance to create their own texts.

NEWSPAPER ARTICLE A

Daughter's voice 'saved my life'

Accident victim Walter Morgan believes that the sound of his daughter's voice saved his life.

Mr Morgan of Alvescot Road, Carterton, was lying unconscious with multiple injuries after a car crash when his daughter, ambulance driver Mrs Maxine Tabberer, arrived on the scene.

Maxine is based at Witney ambulance station and was called to the accident at RAF Brize Norton.

Mr Morgan, 63, said "She called out 'Dad' to me. I thought I had been having a bad dream and she was waking me up.

"I'm convinced that if it hadn't been for the sound of her voice, I would not have woken up and would not be here today.

"I was out cold and apparently my blood pressure was very low. I think her voice brought me round and her presence reassured me. She was wonderful."

Mr Morgan was given oxygen and taken to the John Radcliffe Hospital, Oxford, in Maxine's ambulance. He spent a week in hospital being treated for a broken leg, broken arm and three broken ribs.

The accident with a Land Rover happened as he was returning to work at RAF Brize Norton where he is a senior storekeeper. Mr Morgan, who acts as the 'eyes' for his wife Madge who is a blind bowls champion representing England, is now recovering at home.

His daughter Maxine, who lives in Queens Road, Carterton, said: "It was a great shock when I arrived at the scene of the accident and saw my father lying there.

"He was in a pretty bad way. He didn't come round until I started talking to him, and he was in a state of shock."

NEWSPAPER ARTICLE B

Ambulance girl brings father back to life

It's me, Dad!

By Maria Morris

A brave young ambulance driver on a mission of mercy didn't know she was on the way to save the life of someone very dear.

For when Maxine Tabberer arrived in an ambulance at the scene of a horrific accident she found that the unconscious victim was her own father.

Maxine, of Queens Road, Carterton, was completely stunned... but she knew she had to pull herself together and do her job.

And it was 28-year-old Maxine's gentle voice calling out to her dad that brought him back to life.

Voice

"It was a marvellous miracle," said 63-year-old Mr Walter Morgan of Alvescot Road, Carterton.

"If it hadn't been for hearing my daughter's voice, I probably wouldn't be here today," he said.

Mr Morgan had broken an arm, a leg and three ribs in a head-on collision with a Land Rover. He was on his way back to work at lunchtime, to

RAF Brize Norton where he is a senior storekeeper, when the accident happened. His new Talbot car and the Land Rover were completely wrecked but the other driver was luckily, unhurt.

Maxine, who has worked as an ambulance driver in Witney for nearly a year, was out on a routine call when a radio message asked them to re-route to Carterton for a traffic accident.

"When we were nearly there, another message came, saying something about a close relative. But it just didn't occur to me that it could be mine," she said.

"It was a terrible shock to see my father lying there.

"I quickly went through in my mind what to do and checked for bleeding and fractures.

"I think it was a comfort to him that I was there."

1.10 Using questionnaires

Questionnaires, especially if designed with controversial statements for discussion, can be very effective devices for motivating writers and providing students with content for their individual writing. They provoke response and reaction which can be exploited orally in the classroom as a precursor to writing. Students thus have the opportunity to explore ideas, make selections, and begin organizing their ideas.

LEVEL Lower intermediate upwards

TOPIC A view of education

PREPARATION 1 You will need to prepare copies of the questionnaire overleaf so that students can have individual copies to fill in and use for interviewing.

2 One way of starting a topic on education is to make a collection of newspaper headlines which indicate opinions about how education should be organized or developed. You could copy these for students or paste them on to a wall poster.

"I will educate my own children" says father of three.	Parents defy new education cuts
Ministers review education system	'Bring back caning' says headmaster
Student dropout fears	College Bankruptcy Shock
More nursery places needed	
Teachers defend strike action	Son goes missing from college

IN CLASS

1 Warm up to the topic by selecting some of the headlines, asking students what they indicate and what their own opinion of them is.

2 Hand out the questionnaires and ask students to look at them quietly and individually and to tick 'agree' or 'disagree'.

3 Then ask students to work in pairs. They should exchange opinions and tick their partner's agreement or disagreement in the second column. Encourage them to justify their opinions and say as much as they can.

4 An optional step would be to hold a short class discussion and to elicit opinions, using them to develop useful vocabulary on the blackboard.

5 Ask students to continue working in pairs and to think of some statements they could make for the last section of the questionnaire. Give them a few minutes to brainstorm on this.

6 Get some suggestions from the class for the last section and write them on the blackboard.

7 Students should now have ideas for their own pieces of writing, a composition with the title 'My view of education'.

REMARKS

With a more advanced group, the writing task could be to develop a manifesto for a political party, which sets out the party line on education. This would include making promises and describing future intentions as well as giving opinions. The language of these functions would need to be presented in the questionnaire.

QUESTIONNAIRE

		You		Your partner	
		Agree	Disagree	Agrees	Disagrees
Nursery	1 All children of three years and over should be able to have full-time nursery education. 2 Nursery education should be free. 3 Nursery children should not be at school for more than half the day. 4 Nursery children should learn to read.				
Primary	5 Children should start primary school when they are five. 6 All children should be tested for reading when they are seven. 7 Children should learn to play team sports. 8 Children should sit still and be silent in the classroom.				
Secondary	9 Parents should have the right to send their children to private schools. 10 Parents should pay for their children's books. 11 Schools should not have mixed-ability classes. 12 Physical punishment should be allowed.				
College or University	13 .... 14 .... 15 .... 16				

NOTE: You may make photocopies of this for classroom use (but please note that copyright law does not normally permit multiple copying of published material).

1.11 Working from opening sentences

If a writer wants to become effective and convincing, he or she needs to develop a sense of direction in writing. One way of developing this is in relation to the writing of narratives which particularly need a sense of moving forward from a beginning towards a goal of some kind.

LEVEL

All levels (The task is appropriate to any level if the opening sentences are chosen or written carefully at the right language level.)

TOPIC

Opening a story

PREPARATION

From a variety of novels and short stories, find some interesting or intriguing opening sentences or make up your own. Here are some examples suitable for upper intermediate students:

> I had decided to spend the whole of that Saturday afternoon in Central Park. Little did I know what adventures were about to start.

> It was impossible to keep track of the days, imprisoned in this dark and crowded cell.

> David had come back. He was there, standing in front of me, with that same arrogant look on his face as when I had last seen him.

> That was really the start of it all, when I saw the pattern of my life, how it all added up . . . so that what had been without purpose suddenly became purposeful.

> The plane crossed the coast eighty thousand feet up. Michael Ellis watched the sliding curve of the earth beneath him.

> The girl shaded her brown eyes from the sun, and looked up at the graceful birds wheeling above the ship.

IN CLASS

1 Take one of the story openings and discuss it with the class. Ask them how they think the story could continue. Elicit as many ideas as you can about characters, setting in time and place, and possible events.

2 Ask students to work in pairs and give them some questions to direct their discussion. You could set a time limit to concentrate the discussion. Possible questions are:

- *Which of these sentences do you think is most effective as a story-opener and why?*
- *What sort of story do you think it opens?*
- *How do you think the story might continue?*

3 Hold a feedback session with the class and elicit their opinions. Encourage other students to ask questions of those who volunteer opinions, so that the whole class is involved in discussion.

4 Arrange students in pairs (or in groups of four with other students who chose the same opening sentences). The students make up a plan for the story which develops from the opening.

5 Students then write individual stories, stopping occasionally to read each other's work and give advice. Encourage them to use the outline in a flexible way, elaborating with their own ideas or moving away from the plan if other ideas develop.

REMARKS

Step 3 enables cross-fertilization of ideas in the class at the stage of getting ideas together and planning the content. Step 4 allows for collaborative planning of outlines which are then used in a flexible way by individual students. It is important for them to appreciate that a plan should not be a strait-jacket. Step 5 provides an audience for the writer and another reader's perspective on the possibilities for improvement and rewriting.

1.12 Freewriting

Freewriting is a technique which has the main purpose of generating ideas. It tries to overcome the problem of writer's 'block'. It has sometimes been called speedwriting or quickwriting because its main feature is writing as quickly as possible without stopping. Its other main feature, a product of the speed, is that the writer concentrates on content rather than on form. In this way, the primary focus is on getting as many ideas down on paper as possible. At a later stage, quality can take over from quantity in a process of selection and redrafting.

Freewriting is a useful follow-on activity from brainstorming which can be done as a class or with students working individually. The latter technique is used in the sequence set out below.

LEVEL

Lower intermediate upwards

TOPIC

Learning a foreign language

PREPARATION

No preparation is needed but you should have a blackboard which can be seen clearly by the class, or an overhead projector (OHP) with transparency.

1 Explain to the class that you are going to try out a technique called freewriting, which some writers find useful as a way of 'getting started' and developing ideas for a theme. The theme here is 'Learning a foreign language'.

2 Ask students to brainstorm individually for a few minutes and to jot down their experiences of learning a foreign language, noting anything that occurs to them. Do the same yourself while they are writing.

3 Make yourself a guinea-pig and demonstrate freewriting to your students (or ask a colleague to come in to do it). Choose an item from your jottings and start writing freely and quickly on the blackboard or on an overhead projector transparency so that the class can watch you composing. Try to elaborate on the item you have chosen from your notes. Tell your students beforehand not to interrupt but to stop you after you have covered about ten or twelve lines. This is what I produced when I experimented with my class:

> What I remember most about learning French at school is singing French songs (which were incomprehensible to me) on a Friday afternoon during the lesson, and singing them deliberately out of tune to annoy the teacher. I was about eleven years old then. And I remember a textbook which was full of stories about a silly boy called Toto and his family. I did endless grammar exercises which I didn't understand and always got wrong. I didn't feel very positive about France or French people then. In fact, it wasn't till much later when I visited Brittany, that French began to make sense.

4 Show students how one part of the writing could then be taken to elaborate further as you begin to remember more. I bracketed the part about the singing and went on to produce a further paragraph.

5 Encourage students to try the same process and give them time to work quietly by themselves. When they 'dry up' they should go back to their notes and choose another point to freewrite about.

6 The students should end up with jottings, paragraphs, and partly elaborated points; in other words, a collection of partially drafted pieces of writing which are now ready to be redrafted with an eye to accurate language and organization and development of the theme.

REMARKS

The advantage of freewriting is that is helps students to 'discover' the things they can write about within a general theme. It also obliges students to redraft, thereby highlighting the importance of redrafting in the process of composing. However, the teacher needs to be aware of probable variation of response to this activity. It seems to suit some personalities very well and I found some of my students using it a good deal afterwards. Other writers, including myself, are far less comfortable with it and prefer to think for a good while before putting pen to paper. It is probably best therefore, to introduce freewriting as an experiment and to talk about it as one of a range of techniques which might be useful to the individual writer.

1.13 Creative writing

In my experience there are many students in classes at higher levels who are not doing examinations and who are not necessarily learning English for academic or professional purposes. They enjoy creative writing; and many of those who do have specific purposes for writing enjoy the chance to be more creative. The following task has been used successfully with many different groups.

LEVEL

Intermediate to advanced

TOPIC

'Moon people'

FUNCTION

Describing (a group of people and their habits).

FORM

Creative composition.

FOCUS

Features of an informal, conversational style.

PREPARATION

You need to prepare:
a. copies of a text such as 'Moon people' (overleaf).
b. copies of drawings like those found in Edward de Bono: *Children Solve Problems*. Teachers with a talent for drawing can create their own drawings on large pieces of paper as wallcharts. Miss out the children's explanations.

IN CLASS

1 Show the pictures to the class. Explain that they were drawn by children who were asked to think of ways to improve the human body. Ask students to work in pairs and to take turns at describing the pictures, suggesting what advantages the unusual features give to the person.

2 Hold a short feedback session to see what interesting and amusing suggestions the class can make. Use the session to check vocabulary.

3 Then read out the children's own explanations for the improvements.

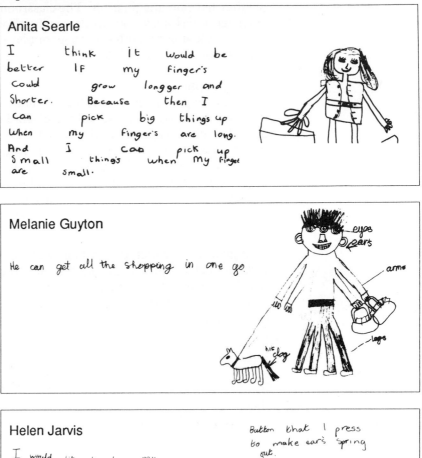

Anita Searle

I think it would be better if my finger's could grow longger and shorter. Because then I can pick big things up when my finger's are long. And I can pick up small things when my finger are small.

Melanie Guyton

He can get all the shopping in one go

Helen Jarvis

I would like to change my ear's
I would like to press a button and my ear's would shoot out
Then I would not have to strain my ears
I thing it would be a good Idea.

Button that I press to make ear's spring out.

4 Give out copies of the passage of your choice. As students read, ask them to underline any expressions which create an informal style. Elicit these and write some on the blackboard. In 'Moon people' these would be phrases such as:

– *I must tell you about . . .*
– *I forgot to mention . . .*
– *I hardly like to tell you . . .*

5 Ask your students to imagine a similar group of beings from folk-tale, legend, or outer space, and to write a similar type of description for homework.

REMARKS

I have always made this an optional activity for homework, as not all students will want to spend time on it and there are some who say they have no imagination. The classroom provides useful language and skills work; for those who choose to complete the writing task at home, it has been a popular source of further comparison and discussion.

TEXT

Moon people

When moon people grow old, they do not die. They just vanish into thin air like smoke . . . and talking of smoke, I must tell you about their diet which is precisely the same for everyone. When they feel hungry, they light a fire and roast some frogs on it . . . for there are lots of these creatures flying about in the air. Then, while the frogs are roasting, they draw up chairs round the fire, as if it was a sort of dining-room table, and gobble up the smoke. That is all they ever eat, and to quench their thirst they just squeeze some air into a glass and drink that; the liquid produced is rather like dew.

Bald men are considered very handsome on the moon and long hair is thought absolutely revolting; but on young stars like the comets, which have not yet lost their hair, it is just the other way round, or so at least I was told by a comet dweller who was having a holiday on the moon when I was there.

I forgot to mention that they wear their beards a little above the knee; and they have not got any toenails for the very good reason that they have not got any toes. They use their stomachs as handbags for carrying things around in for they can open and shut them at will. If you look inside one, there is nothing to be seen in the way of digestive organs, but the whole interior is lined with fur so that it can also be used as a centrally heated pram for babies in cold weather.

The upper classes wear clothes made of flexible, coloured glass, but this material is rather expensive, so most people have to be content with copper textiles . . . for there is any amount of copper in the soil, which becomes as soft as wool when soaked in water.

I hardly like to tell you about their eyes, for fear you should think I am exaggerating, because it really does sound almost incredible. Still, I might as well risk it, so here goes. Their eyes are detachable, so you can take them out if you do not want to see anything and put them back when you do. Needless to say, it's not unusual to find someone who has mislaid his eyes altogether and is always having to borrow someone else's; and those who can afford it keep quite a number of spare pairs by them just in case.

1.14 Writing poetry

Poetry is expressive writing of the most personal kind and, as such, needs careful and sensitive treatment. It should always be an optional activity in general purpose English language teaching with multilingual groups and multicultural backgrounds. The activities I devised below were used with young women aged eighteen to twenty, mostly from European backgrounds. Two friends in the group brought into class some poetry they had tried to write and showed it to me and to others in the group. In response to their interest I made two activities on cards (pasted inside manilla folders) for self-access work. Both activities had been used earlier with fifteen to sixteen-year-olds in secondary school. The examples of students' work show how poetry can motivate students to try out this kind of personal expression themselves.

The type of poem selected for the first activity certainly demonstrates the language of imagination but it is a clear and comprehensible language expressed in a simple form. Writing poems in blank verse gives students the opportunity to explore the language, to organize their ideas with great care, to manipulate sentence structure, to select words, and to think about appropriate collocations. It also encourages the drafting process. The students came to me with drafts for comment and were anxious to make their poems 'sound right'.

LEVEL

Lower intermediate to advanced

TOPIC

A Chinese poem or a shape poem

PREPARATION

The first activity could work with a range of examples of fairly simple poetic forms. I have used Chinese verse in translation as it is possible to find several verses on the same theme as examples. The poems were pasted on one page inside a folder and the instructions pasted on the opposite page.

IN CLASS

1 Take a small amount of class time to introduce the idea of writing poetry, as it may not appeal to all students. The introduction may come naturally by reading a poem which fits into a particular topic. It may arise from studying a poem in class with a suitable group of students who show interest in this.

2 Show students the self-access work card and example of student's shape poem, and invite them for homework to try writing some poetry which you will be glad to look at and make comments on. Let the students borrow the card to take home.

3 Make time available to those students who experiment to bring their drafts to you for advice and comment.

WORK CARD

In Chinese history it was considered a mark of respect for a young poet to repeat the theme of an earlier poet's work, within the same form. One common theme is the thoughts and feelings of a lonely woman who is waiting for her husband or lover to return.

1 Read through the poems below.
2 Can you write a short verse on the same theme?

FAN YÜN

In imitation of 'Since you, sir, went away'[1]

Since you, sir, went away,
My gauze curtains sigh in the autumn's wind.
My thoughts of you are like the creeping grass
That grows and spreads without end.

HSÜ KAN

A wife's thoughts, III[2]

Since you, sir, went away,
My bright mirror is dim and untended.
My thoughts of you are like flowing water;
Will they ever have an end?

WANG JUNG

In imitation of Hsü Kan

Since you, sir, went away,
My golden burner has had no incense,
For thinking of you I am like the bright candle,
At midnight vainly burning itself away.

EXAMPLES

The following are examples of students' poems based on the work card:

Since you sir, went away
The leaves have fallen from the trees
The flowing river has frozen hard with ice
And I am cold and lonely.
                              Brita

Since you sir, went away
My heart is sad and lonely
I walk among pale white lilies
They mirror my melancholy mood.
                              Marie Christine

VARIATION

The level of the class I tried this with was constrained by the example from Lewis Carroll: *Alice in Wonderland* which is quite difficult in terms of conceptual content. In fact, if you use the example of student's work or make up your own simple 'shape poem', the activity could be used very successfully with elementary students upwards.

PREPARATION

As with the first task, make work cards, this time using 'The mouse's tale' from *Alice in Wonderland*, that students could borrow to read and use at home. Alternatively, 'The mouse's tale' can be used in class to show that it is the visual effect which is most important.

IN CLASS

1 Show the students 'The mouse's tale'. It is not even necessary to study it in detail, simply to draw attention to the visual effect. (If students produce shape poems in your classes it is worth keeping copies of them and making a wall display which will interest and motivate new students and classes.)

2 Ask students to work in pairs or groups and to brainstorm for a few minutes, listing things which have distinctive shapes, such as:

– animals
– flowers
– toys
– machines

3 With a suitable class who respond well, it may be worth trying some pair work in class on getting ideas together for the kind of things they might put in the 'poem'. Alternatively ask students to think about it for homework and to explore some possibilities.

4 Encourage students to bring their drafts to you for comment and advice.

5 With the students' permission, a good way to round off this activity is to publish their efforts as a wall display or in the form of a class magazine.

EXAMPLE

The following is an example of a student's shape poem.

tower above the streets and houses down below.
The helicopters greet me as they pass, like
I look   whirring
down   insects.
at   They
the   b
move-   u
ment   z
below   z
me.
To   a
where   w
my   a
feet   y.
stand
hard
against
the
earth.
I
am
a crane.

MajBrit Eklund

NOTE: You may make photocopies of this for classroom use (but please note that copyright law does not normally permit multiple copying of published material).

1.15 Reporting real events

Another way of overcoming the problem of having something to say and getting ready to write is to base the writing on a real event, either national or local, in the outside world, and to give the students the role of newspaper reporters who are collecting information for an article. It may well be the case that there is discussion and reporting in the paper prior to the event and there may be radio and TV coverage as well which the teacher can exploit in the activity. The event chosen for the task below is the London Marathon, which will serve as an example. The steps in procedure will have to be carefully organized over a number of lessons and may form only parts of lessons in which 'setting up' the activity and 'reporting back' take place before the writing workshop, which will take a whole lesson.

The task itself is based on the work of Cliff Jansen, who presented parts of it as a materials assignment while following the Postgraduate Diploma in English Studies for Language Teaching at Ealing College of Higher Education.

LEVEL

Intermediate upwards

TOPIC

The London Marathon

PREPARATION

1 If you can collect material beforehand, you can present it as a collage of maps, pictures, articles, etc. on the wall (see end of 1.15).

2 Prepare the question sheet and information sheet as shown.

IN CLASS

Lesson one
1 Introduce the topic by drawing students' attention to the wall display and ask them:
– *Have you ever taken part in a race or a marathon?*
– *Would you if you had the chance?*
– *Why do you think people enter a marathon?*
– *What sort of people enter?*

2 Having warmed up in this way, ask the students to work in pairs and give them the question sheet, which encourages them to use whatever vocabulary they know.

3 Conduct a short feedback session in which you ask the class for their ideas and write them on the blackboard, checking, explaining, and providing vocabulary as you do so.

4 Tell students they are going to write about the marathon as if they are reporters. Hand out the information sheet and find out what students already know. Ask them to find answers to the other questions as a homework activity. (They can do this by studying the wall display during break times or by looking at newspapers or TV.) Ask the students to form groups of four or five and for each member of the group to take responsibility for finding the answers to certain questions.

QUESTION SHEET

> What qualities do people need to run in marathons?
> How do runners feel during the race?
> Do all runners complete the course?
> Why do some people drop out?
> How do you think it must feel to finish the race?

INFORMATION SHEET

> Event _____
> Date _____
> Sponsor _____
> Number of competitors _____
> Route _____
> Starting time _____
> Last year's winners   Male _____
>   Female _____
> Favourites for this year _____
> _____

Lesson two

1 In a lesson shortly before the Marathon, ask students what they have managed to find out. Organize the groups so that they can collate information in a short exchange session. Then hold a class feedback session.

2 Give the students instructions about what to do before the writing class. They are to choose one of the following ways of writing the report (or any other appropriate ways they might suggest):

a. You can write a general report for a foreign newspaper giving an account of the event and covering many different aspects.

b. You can write about one runner's race from start to finish, and how he or she performed.

c. You can focus on some of the incidents during the race.

d. You were standing on Westminster Bridge. How did the runners look as they crossed the finishing line?

e. You could even write as a reporter who joined the Marathon in order to experience what it felt like to be in the race!

3 Put together those who have chosen to take the same approach to the article, but split groups if necessary in order to keep the group

size down to four or five. Ask the students to discuss whether they want to divide the work in some way, as they are going to write the article together:

– Can someone take notes from the TV news?
– Can another attend the event?
– Can a number collect articles from newspapers (one each)?

The ideal would be for students to attend the event so that they get the feel of it.

Lesson three
This lesson is a writers' workshop with several stages:
a. group discussion in which students collate and discuss the information they have collected;
b. group writing of the article with one person as the 'secretary' or 'scribe' and all members of the group suggesting and arguing out a draft (see task 4.5);
c. checking with you before a final draft is written.

REMARKS

An effective way to conclude this sequence of activities is to add the products to the wall display with a collage of any other information which has been put together.

WALL DISPLAY

The London Marathon

the lucky 28,000

the front-runners

lining up on Sunday

HOW THEY FINISHED

1.16 Interviewing people

LEVEL   **Lower intermediate**

TOPIC   **A holiday jobs report**

PREPARATION   This activity can be undertaken with or without a model text to demonstrate the type of report students might write. Step 3 below is therefore optional. If you want to use a text you need to write or find an appropriate one. Many topics lend themselves to the technique of collecting information and ideas through interviewing other students. Such topics may be:

– a sport they have taken up
– a holiday they have experienced
– their ideas about a future career.

The task below uses the topic of part-time or holiday jobs and is suitable for young adults in full-time education in countries where part-time jobs are possible. The following text is an example of a text you could prepare.

> Winston James, fourteen years old, works at a neighbourhood supermarket on Saturdays. He starts stocking the shelves at eight and, after the store opens at nine, he wheels trolleys out to customers' cars in the car park and sometimes to nearby houses.
> He likes delivering the groceries because he usually gets some tips but he doesn't enjoy stocking shelves so much.
> 'It's easy but boring. I prefer talking to customers.'
> Winston likes working. 'I enjoy earning money, I make £8 a day. I'm saving up for a good camera.'

IN CLASS   1 Introduce the topic of part-time or holiday jobs by asking who in the class has experience of this. Encourage the class to question volunteers about their experiences.

2 Elicit from the class the questions they can ask and the categories these relate to. Build up a chart on the blackboard like the one shown below.

AGE	How old are you?
TYPE OF JOB	What type of part-time work do you do?
EMPLOYER	
PLACE OF WORK	
HOURS	
LENGTH	
ENJOYMENT	
WAGES	
SAVINGS	
SPENDINGS	

3 Read your short model text with the class and use the questions above to check comprehension. Add any other categories generated by information in the text.

4 Ask each student to interview another person in the class using the questions and making notes. Alternatively the task could be done as homework, in which case students could be encouraged to interview friends or members of their families.

5 The notes can then be used as the basis for writing a report.

6 The class's work can be displayed, with photographs of the students interviewed.

REMARKS

If the students do the work at home it does not really matter if they undertake the interviews in their first language. The writing practice itself is in English. Displaying work is a motivating form of publication: if students know that their work is to be 'published' it can create incentives for clear and imaginative work.

1.17 Conducting a survey

This task gives the students something concrete to research and write about, and has the added advantage of generating certain language functions and forms which can be practised within the context of the task. The end result of the writing is a report – valuable practice for those who may become involved in report writing in their academic or professional roles. The students formulate a questionnaire, conduct a survey, and write a report based on the results.

The most flexible approach to the activity is to ask students to organize themselves into groups of four or five to select their preferred topic. You can make suggestions but students often have their own ideas for what to research. My own classes have chosen a wide range of topics:

– Keeping dogs in urban areas
– Banning cyclists from the roads
– Smoking in public places
– Roles and responsibilities in the family
– Provision of nursery education
– The ideal age for a driving licence
– Which party will win the election?
– No right to strike for teachers
– The best eating places in town
– Spare-time activities

LEVEL	**Lower intermediate upwards**
TOPIC	**Surveying social issues**
PREPARATION	During the task it is useful if you can make copies of questionnaires which the students produce. Alternatively, each student could be asked to make several handwritten copies.

IN CLASS

1 Tell the students that they are going to work in groups to make a questionnaire on a subject of their own choice or one suggested by you.

2 Choose an example to discuss with the class. Use it to elicit and discuss the kind of information they want to obtain and what questions they would ask. For example, with the topic 'Banning cyclists from the road', students might consider a first question:

– *Are you a cyclist or a driver or both?*

or

– *Do you think of yourself mostly as a driver or a cyclist?*

Further questions can then be directed at each category, e.g. to cyclists:

– *How often do you cycle?*
– *Where do you cycle?*
– *What are the main dangers for cyclists?*
– *Is there good provision for cyclists?*
– *What do you think of drivers?*

3 The students decide on a topic in their groups, write out their questionnaire and check it with you. Your role at this stage is to monitor the group work, give advice, and prompt.

4 Groups can then carry out a survey using their questionnaires. If they are in language schools in an English-speaking environment, students can interview host families, local contacts, and people in the street. In non-English-speaking situations, they can interview members of their own class and other classes.

FOLLOW-UP

In a follow-up session, groups discuss the information they have managed to collect and write a report of their results, with conclusions. This could be preceded by a presentation from you of the kind of language needed:

– *Almost everybody*	*reported that . . .*
– *The majority of people*	*said that . . .*
– *A minority of people*	*thought that*
– *Only a few people*	*complained that . . .*

1.18 Observing and note-making

The last task in this section is different from the others and a little unusual in the book, and I should like to acknowledge Zubeda Bhagat, a teacher of English as a second language in the London Borough of Ealing, as the originator of this activity. I observed it being used in Britain with a small group of children who were learning English as a second language at the primary level. It was very successful both as a language development task and as a writing development task. As a 'discovery learning' task it also helped the children to develop the skills of observation, note-making, and organization of ideas in description likely to be useful to them in subjects across the curriculum. I have presented it here because many elements, note-making from observation, organization, etc. can be successfully transferred to other EFL situations with older learners.

LEVEL

Elementary (primary)

TOPIC

Small creatures

PREPARATION

Bring into the classroom a snail in a small glass tank so that it can be seen clearly, and closely observed. Place the snail in the tank beforehand so that its movement can be traced by the silvery trail left on the glass. Cover the tank so that the snail is revealed as a surprise.

IN CLASS

1 Uncover the snail, gather the group of children around the tank on the desk and ask the children to describe what they see. Encourage further 'talk' by asking questions and gently guiding the discussion. Below is a transcript of part of the conversation that took place during the lesson I observed.

Teacher	Look at this. Can anyone tell us what it is?
Chorus	A snail . . .
	Snail
	It's a snail . . .
Pupil 1	It's stuck to the glass.
Pupil 2	What's that, miss?
Teacher	What do you think it is?
Chorus	It comes from the snail –
	(pointing) It goes there . . .
Teacher	Yes, it's a trail. The snail made it.
	What colour is it?
Chorus	White, silver . . .
Teacher	Let's touch the snail and see if it moves.
	Now, very gently. It's moving. How does it move?
Pupil 3	I can't see.
Teacher	Can you see any legs?

Chorus   No. It's like a worm,
              but it isn't long.
Teacher And what's this?
Chorus   Shell, a shell . . .
              It's green.
              I've got some shells at home . . .

2 Now draw a chart like the one below on the blackboard and ask
pupils to remember what they discovered about the snail. As they
make suggestions about its colour, appearance, and movement, fill
in words and phrases in the chart on the blackboard.

What colour is it?	What does it look like?	How does it move?
green shell black body	long and flat no legs two feelers eyes at tip of feelers	slowly silvery trail

3 The children can then use the chart to build up their own short
description of the snail.

An example of one pupil's work is shown below. It shows a
developing ability to produce a clearly organized description of the
kind appropriate to 'science' in a general way.

EXAMPLE

The Snail is black and has a green shell. It is long and flat. It has no legs. and it sticks to the ground. It We saw a silvery trail. It has two feelers on its head. He has eyes at the top of the feelers. It moves the feelers to see. The snail is very slow.

2 Communicating

Introduction

Writing in real life is usually undertaken in response to a demand of some kind. For adults, the demand may arise from academic studies, professional responsibilities, or from such social roles as friend, purchaser, enquirer, complainant, or counsellor. Students may have any of these present or possible future purposes for writing in English. But in every case there is a real audience to whom a message must be communicated.

Writing in the English-language classroom can become unreal if it is only ever produced for one reader, the teacher, and if its purpose is limited to enabling the teacher to assess the correctness of the linguistic forms used. Under these conditions students have to imagine contexts for their writing and motivate themselves to write appropriately for the imaginary readers. It is far more motivating for them if their writing can become genuine pieces of communication with real audiences such as other students, visitors, the local newspaper, organizations, etc. Then they can think carefully about the identifiable and particular context which will determine the exact message and style of their written communication.

Jerre Paquette (1982) reports the comments of fifteen-year-old Robert on the impersonality of classroom writing in general:
> 'In school we write . . . not to anyone . . . we just give information. Not to someone . . . we just write information down on paper.'

The problem can be exactly the same for adult writers in a foreign language. Consider the following questions:

1 What writing tasks (whole paragraphs or texts) have you set for your students over the last few weeks?

2 When you set the tasks did you have clear in your own mind what you expected from your students in terms of such features as: level of formality; emotive tone; use of colloquial expressions; use of contracted forms; amount of assumed knowledge in the reader; or degree of explanation in informative or discursive writing?

3 What instructions or examples did you give your students to enable them to meet your expectations?

4 Did you set the writing task in a clear context and provide an audience?

Look, for example, at these three texts which cover the same topic, 'The River Thames'. It is easy to tell from the selection of content, the level of formality in the style, etc., what kind of audience each has been written for. Each would be found in a certain context.

The Thames retains a living role in the life of London and its region; even the dwellers in the far suburbs, in Barnet or in Purley, and in the towns beyond, are in large measure dependent upon the work accomplished along its banks. The Houses of Parliament and the government offices in Westminster and Whitehall stand upon the river's brim, while facing them rise the massive offices of County Hall. Along the former marshlands of Thames-side stand great industrial plants, and through the heart of London ply the tugs with their tows of lighters bringing coal, oil and timber. The Port of London remains the major port of the country. The strength of the forces that create the region and determine its changing character derives momentum from the site on the river-bank at the crossing-place of routes of national, indeed of international, importance. And not only the region but also the whole nation, through its capital, enjoys the geographical advantages of this favoured site for its own internal government and trade and for contact and commerce with Europe and the world beyond.

Our house is quite close to Kew Pier which is where the sightseeing boats arrive from Westminster Bridge – full of tourists who've come to see the Botanical Gardens. Of course, that means it's always busy in the summer – which can be annoying. But, generally speaking, I like living by the river. In fact, I think ours is the best bit of the Thames. When you come, I'll take you to Kew Gardens and to Syon House on the opposite side of the river. There's a very old pub, too, not far away 'The London Apprentice' where we can go for lunch.

And we can take a boat down to Westminster and look at the Abbey and the Houses of Parliament

---

The fascination of a river lies, perhaps, in the variety of activities that it inspires, and the Thames is no exception.

For some – the boatmen and watermen – it is their source of livelihood; for others – the fishermen, yachtsmen, rowers and sightseers – it provides relaxation and pleasure. It's a never-ending bank of resources on which both the amateur and the professional can draw, and yet despite constant use the stimulus never slackens.

While the world rushes noisily and grimly past on either side the Thames flows on, silent and peaceful, providing a graceful setting for the elegant buildings on its banks. Painters like Turner, Whistler, Canaletto and Rowlandson have captured its varying moods and colours, whilst Wren, Barry, Hawksmoor and other architects have been stimulated into designing noble buildings. Writers like Charles Dickens, Thomas Carlyle, Fielding, and George Eliot found near the Thames the atmosphere and the characters they needed; crossing the river are the numerous bridges and tunnels which brilliant engineers Rennie, Brunel, Bazalgette and others were commissioned to design to meet demands for improved communications. Thus the Thames has attracted to itself a variety of unsurpassed skills on which tourists can feast their eyes. Add to this the fact that the Thames has witnessed a succession of momentous historical events and developments and you have one of the great rivers of the world. As long as Europe dominated world history and Britain was master of Europe, so the Thames remained a centre of action. The action is quieter now, less dramatic, but by taking a trip on London's river you will be able to relive some of that past excitement, understand the changes that have occurred over the centuries, and glimpse some of the splendour that is the Thames.

These examples should serve to demonstrate the problems a student would have if asked to write on such a topic without a clear context. Appropriateness becomes impossible. If some of the context which clarifies why students are writing, what kind of text is required, the reader(s) for whom it is intended, and the role relationship between writer and audience (friend to friend, expert to novice, tourist company to sightseer, etc.) is missing, then the writing task becomes artificial and difficult.

Helping students as writers to become aware of their readers and to develop a sense of audience is one of the tasks for a teacher of writing, especially with teenagers who may not have developed this sense in writing their first language. Many adults, too, are not skilled writers in their mother tongue and do not have a mature sense of audience to transfer to their writing in English.

Recent research throws interesting light on this problem for the teacher. Flower and Hayes (1980), investigating the differences between more and less skilled writers, found that skilled writers are sensitive to their audiences. They think about what the reader will be interested in or needs to know by way of background information. Less skilled writers produce what can be called 'writer based' rather than 'reader based' prose; that is, writing which focuses on the topic at the expense of the reader, and as a result is ambiguous and presents ideas and arguments less clearly. Their writing is less accessible to the reader, in that it does not guide him or her through its organization with clear signals as to how the text is developing.

Students, then, need encouragement from the teacher to think about appropriateness as well as correctness in writing. For every piece of writing undertaken, a student needs to answer these questions:
– Who is my reader?
– What do I need to say?
– How can I make it unambiguous and accessible to my reader?

It is a clear sense of audience which enables a writer to select appropriate content and express it in an appropriate form and style, in other words, in a way which facilitates the process of communicating.

It is not easy to formulate meaningful writing tasks which will be read by someone other than the teacher, but the teacher can actually become an audience in a writer-reader relationship involving response rather than assessment. The first two activities described in this section are to do with setting up an exchange of written ideas and opinions between teacher and individual students through letters or journals.

Sometimes it is possible to provide other audiences, depending on the English language 'available' in the environment:

- letters of enquiry to organizations
- letters to the editor of newspapers for publication
- letters of invitation and thanks to guest speakers
- stories for English children or for children who are learning English in an accessible institution
- information leaflets for colleagues in the school or for newcomers to the school
- magazines for publication within the school
- papers and articles for exchange within the group
- scripts for recording or broadcasting as video programmes.

The tasks on the pages that follow give some suggestions for real writing goals for real audiences.

Some items in the list above demonstrate the fact that there is always one possible audience for classroom writing apart from the teacher – the class itself. In the classroom, students can be encouraged to 'share' their writing, showing first drafts to partners for comment and advice, as part of a process of revision. This possibility is taken up and discussed in a later section, *Improving*. Sharing assists writers in that they receive questions and comments on their intentions and on the organization and clarity of their writing. It creates an audience to respond to writing. But care is needed in setting up such activities, especially with less mature or less confident writers. As Donald Graves (1983) puts it, the audience 'can intrude too early on a first draft' or sometimes 'the audience simply says too much'. And he describes the experience of Trevor, a young writer, when he first shared a draft with his five-person writing group. They questioned and commented so much that Trevor dismissed it all and left the group muttering: 'To hell with all of them. I'll do it my own way.'

Class members can also become an audience in quite another way, by using the principle of task dependency. This involves setting up a sequence of activities in which student **A**, Pierre, writes a text for student **B**, Monica, who has to use it in some way to perform a task. The success of Monica's task depends on her understanding of Pierre's writing and her ability to use the information in it. She can criticize and ask for clarification. In this way Pierre has a real reader, someone who has to read and use his writing; he becomes accountable in the way that writers are in real life, and this accountablilty is a strong motivating force for clear and effective writing.

2.1 Exchanging letters with your students

Tasks 2.1 and 2.2 are examples of writing to the teacher as participator.

Herbert Kohl (1977) used the technique of writing letters to his fourth-grade and fifth-grade students. These were mostly bilingual Puerto Ricans learning to write in English. He became a correspondent, a stimulant rather than an evaluator, as he did not correct their letters. But he found that his role as 'language informant' became important, as the students borrowed language from his letters to use in their own. One suggested procedure for using the technique is as follows:

LEVEL

Elementary to advanced

TOPIC

Personal topics

PREPARATION

Prepare a letter, introducing yourself to your students. Tell them a little about yourself, your job, your home, and family.

Mario Rinvolucri (1983) describes an experiment in which he set up such an exchange of letters on a summer course, partly in order to solve the problem of providing a real audience. This is the letter he wrote:

Dear Everybody,
        If we are to work together for two weeks it is important that we get to know each other better. To this end I'd like you to write me a letter introducing yourselves, telling me something about you and your family.
        I live in Cambridge, just north of London. I work for Pilgrims full time. This means that I have to be down here in Canterbury in the summer. The rest of my year is spent either teacher-training in Europe or working on new didactic materials in my home in Cambridge.
        I spend ninety days wandering round continental Europe each year. It's a long time to spend away from home. My wife, Sophie, looks after our two children in Cambridge. Our eldest is a girl, Lola, and our youngest is a boy, Martin, aged 13.
        Please tell me about yourself. Maybe you could give me your letter tomorrow morning.
        Yours,
        Mario.

IN CLASS

1 Suggest that students write the same to you in a letter. On an intensive course you could suggest that they write back for the next day; on a weekly evening course for the next week, and so on.

2 When a student writes to you, reply with another letter responding to opinions and ideas, using your letter to communicate on an adult-to-adult basis rather than as teacher to student.

3 Always treat the letters as a private activity and do not bring them into general classroom discussion. You should not feel obliged to correct them, either. Explain this point of view to students. In fact, students gain language advantages in other ways. Firstly, they get plenty of practice in trying to express themselves in writing, and also gain motivation to make themselves understood. Secondly, your letters provide them with vocabulary, useful grammatical structures, and idiomatic expressions all of which are useful models of language.

REMARKS

The amount of letter writing you do, and its frequency, will have to be worked out realistically in accordance with the size of your class. Mario Rinvolucri reports on the experiment he set up (with six Western European students aged 30–40 on a two-week intensive course) as valuable and exciting, not least because it obliged him to 'spend an hour or more each day thinking about students as individuals, both humanly and linguistically'. The experiment is documented in *ELT Journal* 37/1 in an article entitled 'Writing to your students'.

2.2 Sharing journals with students

The idea of using a writing journal, or a book for writing within English lessons is one many teachers have tried. Like the idea of exchanging letters, described above, it is a device which provides opportunities for writing practice. The main difference is that time for writing is built into a lesson, and all students are encouraged to write for ten minutes or so.

LEVEL

Elementary to advanced

TOPIC

Any personal or learning topic
Jerre Paquette, a Canadian teacher, in his article 'The daily record' in *The English Magazine 9*, outlines the way he has used journals and found them effective with fifteen to sixteen-year-old first language writers, though he reports on their successful use with students aged twelve to sixty. Both principles and procedures, with modifications to suit particular groups, transfer well to adult learners of English. Steps 1–5 below are adapted from his work.

IN CLASS

1 Provide each student with a booklet that is to be considered their personal property with the caveat that it is an essential part of their course and therefore to be made accessible to the teacher but not other students.

2 Tell the students that the booklets remain in a specially designated place in the room and may be taken home only after discussion with you until the end of the course or term, whereupon they go with the student.

3 The students should write in the booklets, on any subject in any style, each day at the beginning of the class for ten minutes only. Extension of this time is occasionally made as the situation demands or permits it (a good writer can usually achieve a whole page in ten minutes).

4 Tell the students the writing is not evaluated or marked.

5 The entries made by the student are responded to in the journals, creating a dialogue-in-writing record and process between student and you (or some partner acceptable to both student and you).

REMARKS

The writing in this activity moves away from writing as an 'assignment' or 'task' towards writing as a more natural exchange of reflections, reactions, and opinions. The teacher becomes a participant and the student initiates the exchange. A journal, in this sense, is a form of communication between two people on topics of their own choice. It becomes a means of experimenting with language.

2.3 Getting to know your group

The next three tasks (2.3 to 2.5) all involve the notion of writing for publication.

The first few lessons of many English language courses often involve the students getting to know each other and the teacher. This can be followed up by a writing task in which each student describes someone else in the group. Often the coursebook in use has a first unit which introduces characters and gives key points of information about them. The descriptions the coursebook provides can be usefully exploited as models for the following writing task.

LEVEL

Elementary to advanced

TOPIC

Our group or our class

IN CLASS

1 Tell students that they are going to interview another member of the group to find out basic information and anything else of particular interest about him or her.

2 Ask students to suggest questions for the interview. Elicit the obvious ones on name, nationality, job, etc., writing up correct question forms on the blackboard or OHP if necessary, depending on the level of English.

3 Then ask your students to think of other things they would like to know (not too personal), and elicit some questions to add to the list. In my own classes the following questions have cropped up:

– *Are you a feminist?*
– *What makes you happy?*
– *Do you support the present government in your country?*
– *Are you optimistic about the future?*
– *Do you support any causes?*
– *Could you live by yourself on an island for a month?*

4 Ask students to conduct their interviews in pairs, giving a minimum of five questions over and above basic information (to ensure range) and an appropriate time limit (to discourage too much focus on one question). Students should jot down notes.

5 Ask students to use their notes to write a short description, selecting information which they think will be most interesting to the group.

6 Let the students read the descriptions of themselves and suggest modifications if they wish.

7 Publish the work by displaying it on the classroom wall as 'Our group'.

REMARKS

This task has other advantages in addition to 'breaking the ice' at the beginning of a course. It introduces the idea that writing can be shared, and suggestions for improvement and modification made by other students. Furthermore, it introduces the idea of 'publication', achieved here through the device of a wall display (see also task 1.15), but also possible through the production of information sheets, brochures, magazines, etc. Publication is one way of providing eventual readers for the writers.

2.4 Making a class magazine

This is particularly suitable for learners in full-time study who are able to devote an hour or a lesson every week to the project. A project can be described as an extended task involving integrated skills work in which writing of a more extensive nature can take place. The great advantage of writing in project work is that, once the teacher has provided a framework and set the task in motion, students can take over, set their own targets, plan their writing, organize themselves into groups, and work at their own pace. The teacher's role is to advise, assist, monitor, and keep up motivation. The project described below, making a class magazine, was undertaken by lower intermediate students, but could be appropriately adapted to any level from elementary to advanced. Further ideas for projects can be found in another book in this series: *Project Work*, by Diana Fried-Booth.

Making a class magazine gives students the opportunity for writing of many different kinds (see the examples), such as reports, stories, reviews, poetry, etc. It also provides an audience – the class itself or the school. The stages necessary for project work writing to be successful are as follows:

LEVEL

Elementary upwards (Examples given are for intermediate students.)

PREPARATION

1 Planning. This is probably best undertaken with you as editor, leading a discussion on the overall format of the magazine and inviting ideas and suggestions for content. Decisions also have to be made on such issues as length, theme, number of sections, etc.

2 Fieldwork. Assign the work to smaller groups, each group allotting tasks to its members. Fieldwork might involve a wide variety of activities inside and outside the classroom, for example, library research on a topic, interviewing, doing a survey, writing away for information, reading something in order to write a review, etc.

3 Writing. As students complete their fieldwork, ask them to begin writing (in pairs, groups, or as individuals) and to call on you for help and advice. You should strongly encourage the students to make revisions before you look at final drafts.

4 Editing. All the students should have the opportunity to see the completed work displayed, for example, across the desks. Let them browse for part of a lesson. They should make general suggestions about the layout of the final product. If the end product is one large magazine (with articles pasted onto card and the card folded to make a 'jumbo book'), then each group can organize its own pages. Otherwise you and the students can elect an editorial panel to produce the edition for photocopying.

5 Publication. If the magazine is available through photocopies or through display in the classroom, readers from the wider 'community' can be invited to write letters to the editor, commenting on articles, etc.

The examples below and overleaf are taken from one class magazine produced in six two-hour lessons, one each week, over half a term.

EXAMPLE A

WINTER

Brilliantly cold, brilliantly frosty,

Streams twinkle, fields sparkle,

Footpaths glint silently,

Sunlit, brittle, silver,

Silver, frosty, silver.

WINTER

Icicles glint coldly,

Frozen footpaths, still trees,

Splendidly bleak, coldly bright.

EXAMPLE B

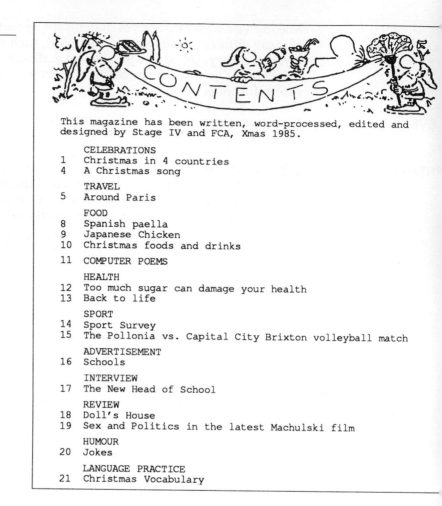

This magazine has been written, word-processed, edited and designed by Stage IV and FCA, Xmas 1985.

CELEBRATIONS
1   Christmas in 4 countries
4   A Christmas song

TRAVEL
5   Around Paris

FOOD
8   Spanish paella
9   Japanese Chicken
10   Christmas foods and drinks

11   COMPUTER POEMS

HEALTH
12   Too much sugar can damage your health
13   Back to life

SPORT
14   Sport Survey
15   The Pollonia vs. Capital City Brixton volleyball match

ADVERTISEMENT
16   Schools

INTERVIEW
17   The New Head of School

REVIEW
18   Doll's House
19   Sex and Politics in the latest Machulski film

HUMOUR
20   Jokes

LANGUAGE PRACTICE
21   Christmas Vocabulary

EXAMPLE C

SPAIN

Xmas and New Year in Spain have become almost a pagan holiday, as in most of the other countries in western Europe. It means two weeks of eating, drinking, buying presents and spending all the money you have saved during the whole year.

However the Spanish Xmas has still got its religious message, people are supposed to share everything with poor people and most of them go to the church on Xmas eve, the 24th of December, and the next day. After the mass, the party starts at night. All the family is together round the table and the dinner is fantastic: fish, salmon, beef, exotic fruits and so on, Then, at midnight, everybody celebrates Jesus' birth. The following day, the whole family goes to church again. The 28th of December is another special day "Dia de los inocentes". Everybody usually plays jokes on each other. It is a funny day.

On the last night of the old year, there is a New Year's party. It usually begins at 10 o'clock, and at 12 o'clock everybody has to eat 12 grapes in the time it takes the clock to strike. If you are able to eat all the grapes, you'll be lucky in the next year. New Year's Day is a catholic celebration as well. The 6th of January, the last day, is the day of the three kings, the Magi. They come to all the houses and leave presents. This custom comes from the three kings who gave Jesus gold, incense and myrhh. On this night, children used to leave food to feed the camels and some "torror" for the kings. The weeks around Xmas mean for most people a holiday break as well.

BACK TO LIFE

A young man from Belgium was trapped overnight on a Swiss mountain in temperatures of minus 5 degrees Celsius. On arrival at the hospital his body temperature was 22 degrees celsius (it is normally about 36.6 degrees celsius) and he showed no signs of life:

>   His temperature was lower than 30 degrees Celsius

>   There was no breathing

>   His pupils were dilated

>   His heart had stopped beating

>   There was no reading on the Encephalogram

The patient was immediately connected to a heart-lung machine which is also used for heart surgery to establish an artificial body circulation.

After two hours on the machine his body temperature had risen to normal. The patient had been brought back to life and needed some days in intensive care.
He suffered no after-effects and the resuscitation was a success.

Adapted from an article 5/11/85 in the "SWISS ROMANDE"
ANITA SIMPSON FCA

2.5 Carrying out mini-projects

This task is set out as an example. Rather than general steps, it will give the precise procedure that was carried out for a large-scale project within which individual students selected mini-projects. Writing was the natural outcome of many of these mini-projects, as you will see in the examples given. The project work was set into the context of a syllabus for summer school learners in an immersion situation. The learners constituted a predominantly monolingual group (German). There were only eight learners in the group, so the teacher was able to give a good deal of individual help with planning, drafting, revising, etc. I am indebted to Ursula Hilton-Jones, who designed this project as part of course assessment for the Postgraduate Diploma in English Studies at Ealing College of Higher Education, and who piloted the materials with her summer school students.

The project revolved around a new shopping centre which has recently been built in the middle of the town where they were staying.

LEVEL

Elementary to advanced (The learners ranged from elementary to advanced and worked together on the projects, forming a supportive learning group.)

TOPIC

A new shopping centre

PREPARATION

The teacher began the project work with some orientation tasks which sent students around the centre to find their bearings and discover what it contained. Each student was given a map of the local area, a blank layout of the shopping centre and a set of instructions for his or her task. Each set of instructions was different, requiring each student to research different aspects from the rest of the class.

Here are some sample orientation tasks:

Basic instructions

You have been given a map of Ealing.
You are staying either at 6 Delamere Road or at 32 Bernard Avenue.
Both addresses are marked in red.

1 Find the street where you are staying.
2 After your arrival, visit the local shopping centre 'Ealing Broadway Centre'. This is the third place which is marked in red on your map.

You have also been given a layout plan of the shopping centre.
Take it with you, also a pen and paper.
If possible go with someone else who has also just arrived.

Basic instructions – variation

1 In the shopping centre locate:
   a. Barclays' Bank
   – find out the exchange rate
      DM – £/FF–£ for selling and for buying.
   – find out the opening times of the bank.
   Take notes.
   b. the chemist's called 'Superdrug'
   c. the sculpture of a horse.

2 Mark the position of **a.**, **b.**, and **c.** on the enclosed blank layout plan of Ealing Broadway Centre.

3 Find Ealing Broadway Station.
Put a √ to show which means of transport you can use from there.

IN CLASS

1 The first step in class was preparation for the project through feedback on the orientation task. This involved sharing of information so that every student could fill in the overall plan of the shopping centre.

2 Students then brainstormed all the possible aspects for investigation and the teacher drew a mind map or 'spidergram' as these were suggested (see Figure 6).

3 Students chose their weekly mini-project on an individual, pair-work, or group-work basis from the plan.

4 The implementation stage took the students outside the classroom into the English-speaking environment for the purpose of information-gathering in connection with their chosen project. Pre-teaching in classroom sessions involved an investigation of the structuring and cohesion of the various text types that students would be producing in their writing. Language items such as structures and vocabulary were 'fed' to students as they needed them in their drafting, rewriting, and editing.

5 During the collation stage, students processed their own notes and information they had collected, e.g. brochures and recordings of interviews with shoppers, residents, etc. They then embarked on their writing tasks. Peer teaching and peer correction played an important role before comment by the teacher.

6 The presentation stage came at the end of each week, when final versions were offered to the group, which acted as an audience for discussion, evaluation, and comment. Each student reported orally on his or her project, its problems, its stages, and its outcome.

7 The reflection stage came at the end of the course when each student was provided with a folder containing all the project work of the group from the complete course. Each student was thus assured of a real readership for the projects and was supplied with models of different text types to draw from in future writing.

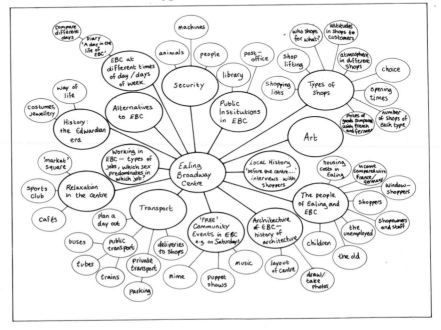

Figure 6

The following examples are some of the work produced. You will see that variety of text types was encouraged. Those shown here include a comparison and contrast of two window displays in shops, guidebook information for a sports centre, and general information on the area.

EXAMPLE A

The Sport places in EBC

for my mini project, this week, I am writing about the sports clubs in EBC.

Are you looking for a place where you can relax, enjoy yourself and take care of your body?
There is a fantastic club — easy to find called 'Stripes Squash and Health Club' in a quiet area of London.
Here you can practise many sports like gymnastics, classic dance, keep fit exercises or squash.
There are nearly 100 classes every week and each is directed by a Studio Manager Teacher. She advises you about the correct exercise programme to suit your needs. She has been teaching for 10 years.

EXAMPLE B

EALING
what to do and what to see

General Information
Ealing is a large suburb in the West of London with 300,000 inhabitants. Besides Ealing is called 'Queen of the Suburbs' because everywhere there are trees in the streets and there are big parks and a common

Parks
There are three big parks in Ealing The most important parks are Gunnersbury Park and Walpole Park. In Gunnersbury Park you can find a museum. There you can see a collection of objects from different centuries. But if you don't want to visit the museum you can do a number of sports. I will give more facts about sporting facilities there in the section about Sports.

EXAMPLE C

EALING BROADWAY CENTRE

Before the Ealing Broadway Centre was built a lot of poor people lived in ruins in this areas
Some designers had thought about what could be built in this place for a long time. But they hadn't got the same ideas but they were agreed that there should not be a grey cold building.
Finally the following plan was chosen:
In the 500,000 square feet big area a centre should be built which should consist of seventy plus shops, offices, a library, a squash and health club, night club and cocktail bar, restaurants and cafes and a car park. A lot of shops changed their position from the main Road to the new building.
Work began in 1980 and finished in 1985. The Ealing Broadway Centre was opened by the Queen on March 7th, 1985.
The developement cost £60m and is one of the largest developments which ever got finished in Britain.

2.6 Giving directions

Tasks 2.6 to 2.11 all involve writing with task-dependency.

LEVEL

Elementary to intermediate

TOPIC

A letter of invitation

PREPARATION

Find a fairly large scale, clear, and readable street map of the local area, for display on the wall or, if you have sufficient copies, for students to use in pairs.

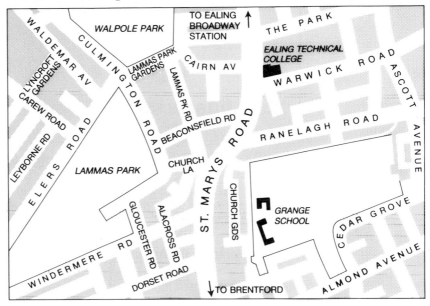

IN CLASS

1 Divide the students into pairs. Ask each student to locate a place on a street map which is his or her real or imagined home. The most important thing is that the student's partner should not have the information.

2 Ask one partner in each pair to write a letter to the other, sending a supper or a party invitation which includes directions to his or her home. The address should be written without the street or number.

3 The directions should begin with reference to a landmark which is clearly marked on the map, for example, 'Get off the bus outside the Hotel Metropole' or 'When you come out of the station . . .'
4 Then ask each student to give the letter to his or her partner to trace the directions on the street map and name the destination.

REMARKS

Here there is an element of task-dependency, as the destination cannot be located without clear directions. The task is particularly useful for students who have just arrived to study in a new town, as relevancy increases motivation. An example of one student's work, based on the map follows.

EXAMPLE

Ealing, London W5

Dear Hosein,

Would you like to come to supper with my family at home on Sunday about 8 o'clock? It would be good if you would come.

It isn't difficult to get to our house. If you come from Brentford get off the bus at the stop opposite the Ealing College (Technical College) at the corner on Warwick Road and St. Mary's Road. Walk a short way back and turn right into Beaconsfield Road.

This will bring you to Lammas Park Road on the right. At the end of this road there is Lammas Park Gardens on the left. Walk along here with the park on the right side until you come to the main road. Cross the main road and our road is directly opposite. Our house is number 28 on the right, just after Carew Road. I hope you can come.

Best wishes

Ariane

2.7 Jigsaw story writing

The use of picture stories to stimulate narrative writing in EFL is well established. This task uses a picture story and the principle of the information gap to create task dependency. An information gap task is basically one where one student or group of students holds information which is unknown to another student or group. This simulates real life where communication frequently involves the passing on of previously unknown information from one person to another. In this task each student has only one picture from the sequence and students are required to 'pool' their knowledge in order to piece the story together.

LEVEL   **Elementary to upper intermediate**

TOPIC   **Caught in the act!**

PREPARATION   Prepare one or several copies (as many copies as there are groups in step 4 below) of the picture sequence. The picture sequence(s) should be cut up into single pictures for distribution to individual students. For this example we will assume a group of fifteen students.

IN CLASS   1 Put your students into groups of three.

2 Give each group or individual in a group one of the pictures, so everyone in the group has the same picture to discuss and write about. The diagram below shows the arrangement of the groups.

| picture A | picture B | picture C | picture D | picture E |

Figure 7

3 Working together within their group, students write a paragraph describing events in their picture. In order to ensure coherence, it is wise to suggest that everyone works in the past tense. When the paragraph is agreed and completed each student writes down his or her own copy.

4 Collect the pictures. Then reorganize the class into groups of five, each student having a description of one picture/part of the story. The rearrangement can be shown diagrammatically as follows:

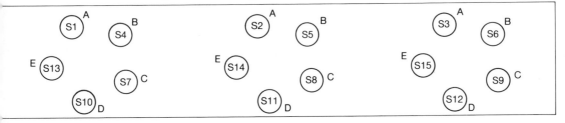

Figure 8

5 Ask the students to assemble the parts into a narrative, making necessary modifications to produce a logical story with appropriate cohesive devices, tense sequences, etc.

6 A final stage could be reading the completed versions out loud to compare and assess them. Below is an example of an appropriate picture sequence.

EXAMPLE

NOTE: You may make photocopies of this for classroom use (but please note that copyright law does not normally permit multiple copying of published material).

2.8 Asking and giving advice

Almost a traditional activity in EFL classrooms, writing letters to an agony column can be modified into pair or group work in order to provide an audience for writing, and a sequence of activities which work on the task-dependency principle.

LEVEL

Intermediate to advanced

TOPIC

Letters to an agony aunt

PREPARATION

You need to have ready examples of letters to agony aunts. In many Western countries, readers can send letters to magazines relating their problems to so-called experts who publish replies. The problems range across a variety of personal, medical, domestic, marital, and professional problems. Here are some examples:

On the Scent

I am 18 and my girlfriend is 17. She's really beautiful and has a lot of admirers. The problem is she wears this horrible perfume. Other people have noticed it too. What can I do?

Have you told her you don't like it? If not, why not? Are you perhaps worried that if she feels criticized she will go off with someone else? It is important to realize that people will respect you for giving your own opinion, even if they don't agree with you. Have the courage of your convictions!

So Lonely

I'm 51, and when my husband left me a year ago for a younger woman, I felt desperate - very frightened, jealous, and angry. Now I have a new job and my confidence is beginning to come back. But I still feel very lonely and panicky at times. I so much want to share my life with someone, but all my friends and work colleagues are married and have their own lives to lead. Can you advise me?

Starting again and building a new life for yourself is difficult at any age. Now that your confidence is returning, do you feel like giving some of your time to others? Your local library will have lists of organizations needing voluntary helpers. There are certainly clubs in your area for divorced and separated men and women. You don't say what your interests are, but I'm sure that with some thought and exploration you will find something to occupy you and make you feel less lonely and isolated.

Peace of Mind?

Since I got married my in-laws have resented me and treated me with suspicion. When my marriage started to break up, my husband told my mother-in-law something about my past which I am ashamed of now. Since then she has never spoken to me. But my husband never told her about some of the awful things he has done. Now my mother-in-law is dying and I don't want her to go thinking I'm a baddy. Should I tell her?

I understand how you feel, but is there anything to be gained from telling your mother-in-law about her son's wrongdoings? You may be wanting to justify yourself at the expense of an old lady's peace of mind. If she dies thinking her son is perfect, is that going to hurt you? You know the truth, and that is what matters.

IN CLASS

1 A preparatory stage is needed in which you and the class discuss the concept of an agony column and reactions to it. Examples like those above can be used with students to whom the cultural concept is unfamiliar. Or you may use them as a reading activity to warm up to the writing and to provide models for the language.

2 Ask each student, pair, or group to think of a problem and formulate a letter to an agony aunt. This second step can be done individually by students or in pairs or small groups.

3 When the students have completed the letters they exchange them with another student, pair, or group whose task is to think of/ discuss possible answers, and write a reply in the role of agony aunt.

4 The letters could then be published on a wall display or put together in a folder in the classroom for students to read.

The advantages of putting students into a group for writing are discussed in *Improving*, tasks 4.5, 4.6, and 4.7. This writing task is particularly appropriate for practising the language function of giving advice.

2.9 Writing letters of invitation

Another, by now almost traditional, task in EFL classrooms is to ask students to fill in a diary as a basis for language practice in giving, accepting, and declining invitations. It is normally used for oral practice of the function of inviting and of the use of the present progressive tense ('I'm sorry I can't . . . I'm meeting my sister for lunch on Wednesday.') but it can be modified into a writing activity involving an information gap and task-dependency.

Elementary to intermediate

A date

You can either copy the page of a week from a small diary for each student or ask your students to draw something similar for themselves.

1 Ask students to fill in the blank pages of their diaries with a number of appointments, real or imagined. You can specify the number if you wish, but the aim is to have a sufficient number so that two students may well have simultaneous engagements. Students should not see each other's diaries, so that an information gap is created.

April	April
17 Sunday *8pm train to Manchester*	**21** Thursday
18 Monday *10a.m. Meeting at Hawes & Son Manchester 2 p.m. train to Oxford*	**22** Friday *8pm. dinner at Tom & Susan's*
19 Tuesday *1 pm lunch with Mary*	**23** Saturday *4p.m. tea at Mother's*
20 Wednesday *8pm theatre*	Notes

2 Ask your students to work in pairs. All the students should write a letter to their partners inviting them to do something the following week.

3 The letters can then be exchanged, and the students read the letters they have received and check in their diaries to see whether or not they are able to accept the invitation.

4 The students individually write a reply, accepting or declining the invitation. If they cannot accept, they should suggest an alternative arrangement.

REMARKS

Versions of this activity appear in various materials and teachers' handbooks. I am not sure of the original source. It is clearly demonstrated in the British Council film: Pair and Group Work in a Language Programme. The accompanying booklet gives a lesson plan for oral practice which might precede the task above.

2.10 Matching descriptions to pictures

LEVEL

Elementary to intermediate

TOPIC

Wanted persons

PREPARATION

You will need a set of pictures of people cut out from magazines. If you want to keep these as a permanent resource, then it is wise to paste them onto card. Pictures should be chosen for clarity, a degree of distinctiveness in the characters, and should ideally show more than just the face or head, that is, some indication of clothing would be useful. You also need your own written description of one of these 'wanted people'. For example, 'Police are looking for . . .'. This could be in the form of one large copy for wall display or individual copies for students.

IN CLASS

1 Take one of the pictures for preparatory work with the whole class. Display it for students and elicit adjectives, descriptive phrases, and sentences for describing the person shown. Ideally this task should follow work on the language for describing people and this stage should therefore be revision. Ask students to focus on distinguishing features. Write words and phrases on the blackboard or OHP.

2 Use the language collected in this way to write a description with the students, asking them to suggest a logical organization, and the structure of sentences, etc. Alternatively, hand out copies of your prepared description as a model, or display a large copy on the wall with the picture.

3 Give each of the students one of the pictures, asking them to keep it concealed from the other students. They should then write a similar description, picking out distinguishing features.

4 Collect in the pictures and completed descriptions.

5 Display all the pictures on the wall and number them.

6 Shuffle the descriptions and give them out to students, ensuring that every student has someone else's text.

7 Students then try to match the descriptions with the pictures, the writer confirming or clarifying.

REMARKS

The task can be adapted according to the size of the group and the availability of resources. The number of pictures should probably be restricted to ten, as higher numbers make the matching task difficult. With larger classes group writing could be employed.

With a small group and computer, the word processing facility can be exploited for step 2, as revision is easily undertaken in writing the description. It has the advantage of showing students the revision process concretely at work.

2.11 Describing and drawing

LEVEL

Elementary

TOPIC

Furnishing a flat

PREPARATION

You need to provide a plan of an unfurnished flat, either individual copies (two for each student) or drawn on the blackboard or OHP for students to copy.

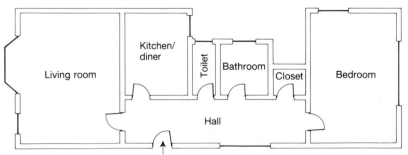

NOTE: You may make photocopies of this for classroom use (but please note that copyright law does not normally permit multiple copying of published material).

IN CLASS

1 Ask each student to 'furnish' the flat, drawing in the items of furniture, then to write a description of the flat, carefully setting out where the furniture is in each room.

2 Students exchange descriptions with a partner.

3 The partner reads the description carefully and uses it to draw the arrangement of furniture on another blank plan. If the writing is not clear and anyone is unsure about the plan, they should check with the writer and ask for clarification.

REMARKS

In real life, people would rarely write such a detailed description, even in a letter to a friend describing a new flat. Here, the activity has a language focus, that is, prepositions and 'There is . . . There are . . .' rather than an authentic writing focus, but the accountability set up in the task ensures that students think carefully about clarity and correctness in sentence structure, an important skill in writing.

2.12 Writing a newscast

The next two tasks (2.12 and 2.13) are concerned with writing for performance.

LEVEL

Elementary to advanced

TOPIC

The News

PREPARATION

1 You will need a recording of the news with several items of reasonable length.

2 Depending on the level of the group and the degree of guidance which you think is necessary or desirable, you will also need one of the following:
– a set of newspaper headlines
– items from the 'news in brief' section of a paper
– a set of short newspaper articles.

BRITONS FELLED

Two British tourists were killed in a village in Brittany when lightning struck a tree which collapsed on their car. Sarah Jones and Fred Wilkins were returning home from a friend's wedding when the tragedy occurred.

DEATH TOLL RISES

The number of people feared injured in the Catsbridge football riots is now estimated at 18. Police are asking for people to come forward if anyone they know is missing.

MAN SOUGHT

Police are looking for John Smith, 31, of Milton Keynes, to help them in their enquiries into the death of 13-year-old Natasha Fielding in a hit-and-run accident on the outskirts of the town last September.

PLANE CRASHES IN FOG

A light aircraft crashed in the Brecon Hills yesterday afternoon when the pilot went off course and ran into freak fog. The pilot, Derek Ford, was able to crash land in a field, and escaped unhurt.

Baby missing in fire

Murder victim identified

Mother's grim ordeal

Doctors plan protest strike

N CLASS

A listening task precedes the writing in this activity.

1 Put on a recording of the news and ask the students to analyse the organization of each item, listening for possible types of content, such as the events as they happened, background to the events, contrasting reported comments of participants or observers, and possible future developments.

2 Explain to the students that they are going to prepare the scripts for a local or national news broadcast. Which of these you choose depends on your students' interests and how well informed they are.

3 Ask your students to work in pairs or small groups so that you have a reasonable number of items for the broadcast.

4 Use one of the prompts suggested above to get the groups started. Headlines may be sufficient, one for each group; 'news in brief' items give a little more idea of content. It may be necessary with some groups to use short articles for a note-taking exercise, picking out key points of information and using them (once the articles have been removed) to write a script.

5 Each group should discuss and agree the content and organization of their item, and then write out the script. You, meanwhile, can monitor and give language help.

6 The completed scripts should be broadcast, the sophistication of the broadcast depending on available facilities. Your students might like to:
a. act out a panel of news readers at the front of the class, one reader elected from each group;
b. make a cassette recording which can be played back for comment (and possibly remedial work);
c. create a video recording which can be shown to the class.

REMARKS

This activity is a useful follow-up to work on reported speech. It also integrates well into a topic on media. In fact, the task can be expanded considerably into a larger project involving discussion of news items, auditions for newsreaders, etc. which would successfully integrate all the language skills.

2.13 Writing a play

Writing a playscript is hardly a realistic writing activity except for aspiring playwrights, but it is motivating and enjoyable, it practises dialogue writing (a requirement for some public examinations), and it is writing for performance. This increases the significance of revision to produce a 'polished' product. It also creates a real audience.

LEVEL

Intermediate to advanced

TOPIC

Family life

PREPARATION   The idea for content might arise in several ways:

    a. from the characters or an episode in the main coursebook;
    b. from events in a newspaper article;
    c. from the narrative of a class reader.

Alternatively you can introduce a group of characters and an episode in their lives which students can build on.

IN CLASS   1 Show students a set of pictures, characters in the play, by displaying them on the wall or blackboard. Invite students to 'design' personalities for them. This can be undertaken as whole class work if you wish the class to have a common group of characters, and for groups within the class to write different episodes of the same play.

If you want to give students more freedom and let each group write their own playlet, then set up this first phase in three steps:

    a. whole class work to set up the activity, discussing one character together;
    b. small group work in which students build up their own characters;
    c. whole class work in which you ask students to describe their characters and compare the descriptions.

2 Give the students the script of one episode in a play. The example opposite is of the first scene of a play and there is a language task accompanying it.

3 The script can be used in a number of ways: to demonstrate colloquial language; to show the conventional layout; to practise language items such as exclamations, tag endings, etc. which are important aspects of informal speech; or for dramatic reading.

4 Ask students to work in small groups and to write a scene from later in the play. They can add new characters if they wish. Ask students to organize their groups with a secretary.

5 Suggest that students discuss the scene and its events first, before trying to write out the script. They should then make a first draft, with the secretary writing down the script as it is worked out. Students may like to take 'parts' as they write.

6 When the scene is complete, ask students, as you move around monitoring the groups, to revise, improve, and edit it carefully.

7 When the groups are satisfied with their version, they should ask you to check it or pass it to another group for comment.

8 The final stage would be for a each group to do a dramatic reading of their own scene, with comment and evaluation from the class if you feel that this is appropriate.

EXAMPLE A

Here is an example of one 'family' group.

Mother
worries about her children

Father
quick tempered

Grandad
elderly

Sandra
easy-going

Chris
responsible

Michael
cheeky

*confused   lively   good-natured   serious   anxious
impatient   cheerful   kind   forgetful   impulsive
generous   sympathetic   quiet   mischievous   caring
understanding*

EXAMPLE B

An English home. The scene is set in the kitchen. It is eight o'clock on a weekday morning. Michael is eating his breakfast. Grandad is reading the paper. Mother is in the hall, calling upstairs.

Mother: Sandra! It's eight o'clock. Are you ready yet? You said Chris was picking you up at eight, didn't you?

Sandra: I'll be down in a minute.

Mother: _____, no one in this family can get up. If I stayed in bed as long as you all do, nothing would get done.

Michael: The world would come to a full stop . . .

Mother: _____, Michael. That's enough cheek from you. Finish your breakfast.

Grandad: Where are my glasses? I can't read the newspaper without my glasses.

Michael: The cat's wearing them.

Mother: _____, Michael, that's enough. You're not sitting on them, are you, Dad?

Grandad: No, _____ not. I'm not stupid, am I?

Mother: Let's have a look. Come on, get up.
(Grandad gets up. He's been sitting on them.)

Grandad: _____, who put them there, I'd like to know.

Michael: Probably the cat.

Mother: I won't tell you again, Michael.
(A car horn sounds outside. Mother walks to the bottom of the stairs.)
Sandra, Chris is here. You don't want to be late, do you?
(Sandra appears at the top of the stairs.)
There's some toast for you on the table.

Sandra: *(rushing through the kitchen)* _____, I just haven't got time.

Mother: _____! You can't go to College without any breakfast.

Sandra: _____. I'll get something in the students' cafeteria. See you later.

Mother: What time will you be home today?

Sandra: Not late, but I'll be going out again. Chris is taking me to a party at Westwood.

Mother: Westwood! That's miles away. Have you asked your father?

Sandra: Bye, Mum, bye, Michael, bye, Grandad . . .

TASK SHEET   Choose the right words and phrases to fill the blanks in the script.

surely not	of course
honestly	sorry
really	don't worry
watch it	well

Now say what feeling or attitude each word or phrase expresses. Choose from this list.

impatience   disapproval   irritation
indignation   surprise   apology
anxiety   reassurance   disappointment
anger   pleasure   fear

2.14 Writing to real people

Sometimes opportunities arise for students to write to real people. Teachers in non-English-speaking environments may be hard-pressed to find such opportunities. They can encourage learners to write letters of enquiry about language courses, summer schools, and holidays, or to write letters to the authors of English teaching materials, graded readers, etc. with comments and opinions, or to find a pen-friend through an appropriate association. But the main audiences for students' writing will probably remain the teacher and the peer group. However, students learning in an English community can be encouraged to exploit the possibilities around them. To take one of the possibilities suggested in task 1.8, newspapers and magazines are full of advertisements, large and small, which invite readers to write for further details. The small ads often provide a number of opportunities for students to write simple letters of enquiry.

LEVEL   **Elementary to lower intermediate**

TOPIC   **The small ads**

PREPARATION   You need to collect an assortment of general and specialist
                     newspapers and magazines, and to bring to class a prepared letter of
                     enquiry as a model. You also need to ask students to bring an
                     envelope and a stamp to the lesson.

IN CLASS   1 Take an interesting advertisement or a small ad and discuss its
                     content and language (abbreviations like s.a.e. and cat., and so on)
                     with the class.

                     2 Elicit from the class what needs to go into a letter of enquiry and
                     derive a simple functional structure, such as saying where the
                     advertisement was seen, expressing interest, giving any necessary
                     personal information, asking for further details, indicating enclosed
                     s.a.e., etc.

                     3 Show the class your model letter and point out the important
                     aspects of layout, appropriate endings (Yours faithfully, etc.).

                     4 Give students ten minutes to browse through a newspaper or
                     magazine to find an advertisement of interest. This period usually
                     becomes a useful skim-reading session with you acting as language
                     and culture informant.

                     5 When students have selected an advertisement, monitor them as
                     each one writes a letter.

REMARKS   I have found that the majority of students are keen to send off their
                     letters though some may opt out and just use the task as a classroom
                     exercise. It is particularly motivating for students who have just
                     arrived in Britain to discover that they can write a real letter in
                     English and receive information of personal interest as a result of it.
                     The letters and brochures they receive are in themselves useful
                     authentic reading materials and may give rise to further
                     correspondence.

3 Crafting

Introduction

In *Composing* we looked at writing from the point of view of 'authoring', in other words, at the *process* which takes a writer from the stage of pre-writing to producing a final draft for a specific purpose and a specific audience. Successful authoring seems to imply having a sense of purpose, a sense of audience, a sense of direction, and a sense of development. However, a focus on authoring need not preclude attention to another, equally important aspect of writing, which could be called 'crafting'. By this we mean the way in which a writer puts together the pieces of the text, developing ideas through sentences and paragraphs within an overall structure.

In order to appreciate the skills needed for successful crafting it is useful to look at finished pieces of writing and to see how ideas are put together and developed. Analysing the *products* of writing will help us to understand a number of things:

1 what features a piece of writing has. In other words, what it is that students are expected to produce when they write;

2 the range of writing and the way one form differs from another, e.g. how a personal letter differs from a formal letter, how a report differs from a memorandum, or how a review differs from an academic article;

3 how one form of writing, such as an academic essay, can vary in overall organization and development according to the specific purpose for which it is written – whether it is to describe a process, debate an issue, compare two systems, etc.

Linguists have only recently begun the task of analysing the features of written texts. However, a brief look through published materials for teaching writing shows that the results of such analyses are already being applied in the design of tasks.

We can take the letter that follows and analyse it to demonstrate the major features of written texts. Awareness of these can inform our approach to the design of writing tasks in the classroom.

25 Woodford Road
Oxford OX4 3RZ
May 6th 1988

The Letters Editor
Radio Times
35 Marylebone High Street
London W1M 4AA

Dear Sirs,

1   I watched the first episode of Strong Poison and was enthralled. My
family was too. Hearty congratulations to all concerned with its
production. I appreciate their meticulous attention to the spirit of
Dorothy Sayers' writing. The period sets were a joy to behold and
5   the casting of the characters was inspired. Edward Petherbridge was
the perfect Lord Peter Wimsey. He had thought himself into the complex
nature of the character with quiet skill. The man was Lord Peter
to the life – in voice, manner, and appearance.

However, I have just a few criticisms to make. Firstly, Harriet was
10   too pretty. And Bunter should not have been so young and
distinguished-looking. Secondly, Lord Peter's hats were about two
sizes too large for him. It was not usual for the rim of bowler
hats to rest on the ears. His trilby and his golf cap looked
similarly excessive. This must have been intentional since the
15   costume department cannot have made the same mistake three times
over. Was the director being faithful to some suggestion in the
book which I never noticed?

Yours faithfully
D. R. Castleton

P.S. 'Strong Poison' is my favourite Sayers story. Do you plan to dramatize
any other ones?

Analysis of this letter brings to light a number of features:

1 Form

The immediately noticeable feature of this piece of writing is its
layout, which relates to the conventions of a letter as a form.
Different forms may have distinctive layouts. Minutes, memos,
technical reports, or academic articles all have different forms
which may need to be learned, and teaching the forms can be one
aspect of a writing course.

2 Discourse organization

If we look beyond the form we see that the function of the text is to give a critical review and this determines how the information is organized into paragraphs and these develop the whole text. This is a brief and relatively simple piece of writing with a paragraph of positive comment and one of negative criticisms. Longer texts may have much more complex overall structure (see tasks 3.4 and 3.5). Classroom writing tasks can make explicit reference to different types of discourse organization and consciously develop students' understanding of how ideas can be developed to create a coherent piece of writing.

3 Paragraph structure

Effective pieces of writing usually show a clear paragraph plan, each paragraph with a topic sentence leading into support sentences which develop the topic. For example, the topic sentence, 'I have just a few criticisms to make' leads into more detailed criticisms and comments. Paragraphing for some writers is an uncertain activity, especially where complex information is carefully developed throughout a longer text. Trimble (1985) makes the distinction between the conceptual paragraph and the physical paragraph and this distinction can be usefully applied to the text opposite and in general terms be helpful to EFL students. By conceptual paragraph he means all the information presented by the writer to develop a particular point, idea, or generalization. However, the conceptual paragraph may be realized in several physical paragraphs. For example, the first paragraph of the letter could actually have been set out as two paragraphs with the divide occurring at 'inspired./ Edward Petherbridge . . .' In this way the conceptual paragraph, commending all the merits of the drama, could have been realized in a first paragraph on the production and a second paragraph on the acting of the major role.

4 Cohesive devices

Cohesive devices are the means by which parts of a text are linked as logically related sequences. They signal the relationship between ideas in such a way that the writer's intentions are made clear. They make obvious the developing thread of meaning which the writer is trying to communicate and often help us to anticipate what is coming next. These links include a variety of devices such as the use of pronouns, articles, conjunctions, demonstratives, prepositional phrases, synonyms, and repetition of key words. Halliday and Hasan (1978) identify a number of cohesive devices which can be seen in the letter:

a. Reference
    A common way of linking ideas across sentences is through back reference by using *it*, or *this*, or *he/she*. Pronouns and demonstratives are the most common reference words in English. They may refer to one word or (as in line 13) to several sentences. Adverbs can create links too, like *similarly* in line 14 which implies a comparison with something mentioned earlier.

b. Conjunction

Classifying these connective devices is made difficult by the fact that many have grammatical functions as well as logical ones. They not only link parts of the text but also make clear the logical nature of the connection, for example, comparison or addition. It would be helpful to students to make this distinction clear by introducing an initial classification by grammatical function. For example:

- co-ordinating conjunctions such as *and* on line 4, which link independent clauses
- subordinating conjunctions like *since* on line 14, which link a subordinate clause to an independent one
- conjunctive adverbs like *However* on line 9, which have no grammatical function but which indicate logical relationships such as time sequence, cause and effect, addition, or opposition.

Classifying in this way to begin with enables students to appreciate grammatical restrictions. They learn to recognize that the use of different conjunctions requires different sentence structure and punctuation. To take a case in point, *In addition* usually comes at the beginning of a sentence and is followed by a comma; *too* usually comes at the end, as in the second sentence of the letter.

A second stage of teaching could then involve classifying the cohesive links according to function: *and, too, in addition, moreover, furthermore, another point is* . . . are all to do with the function of addition. Many materials now give lists of these; what is also needed is thorough practice in using them effectively in the context of writing texts.

c. Substitution

Sometimes a word or phrase substitutes for an earlier item in the text in order to avoid repetition. This can be seen in the postscript where 'ones' substitutes for 'Sayers stories'.

d. Ellipsis

This refers to the omission of words and phrases. For example, in the second sentence of the letter, 'was too' can only be understood if we refer back to the full form in the previous sentence, 'was enthralled'.

e. Lexical relationships

The repetition of words and phrases or the careful choice of synonyms or similar expressions can create unity in a piece of writing. The letter demonstrates it in the sequences:

Edward Petherbridge . . .   the man . . .
Lord Peter Wimsey . . .   the character . . .

5 Choice of vocabulary

Another significant aspect of the letter is the author's selection of vocabulary to create the desired effect. Particularly noticeable is the succession of exaggerated expressions: *enthralled, meticulous, a joy,* and *perfect* which echo through the congratulations and create a superlative impression of the drama.

It is clear from even these brief examples that successful crafting requires the skills of organizing sentences into paragraphs, using linguistic cohesive devices, punctuating meaningfully, selecting appropriate vocabulary, and organizing ideas into a coherent piece of discourse.

English language learners appear to have problems in many of these areas. When we look at our students' writing, some of the problems are clearly to do with the unfamiliarity of the language itself. The obvious example, one which often leaps out from the page, is uncertainty with grammatical structures. Other problems, however, relate to the features listed above. Students may use an unclear cohesive tie. For example, instructions written by a Swedish pharmacist for the use of a nasal spray included the following:

> Three times daily for seven days only, except the condition deteriorates.

Many native speakers would interpret 'except' as 'unless', prefacing the condition that if you feel worse you can carry on with the treatment. In fact the meaning intended was 'otherwise' indicating the warning that if you use the nasal spray for more than seven days it will actually cause a worsening of the condition.

Other problems in writing might prove less dangerous to the reader but equally confusing. Students may use appropriate cohesive devices in terms of meaning but not realize their syntactic constraints and place them wrongly, use incorrect punctuation, or over-use them. This student has fallen into all three traps:

> People who live in the country, whereas, have a pleasant environment. On the contrary town dwellers suffer from noise and furthermore cramped conditions.

Paragraphing is another potential problem area. A student's work may consist of long strings of sentences with no 'natural breaks', so that it is difficult to see the relationship between main and subsidiary points or to anticipate changes in topic.

Rivers and Temperley highlight another hazard, one which relates to transfer from the first language, that is, the tendency to produce long, rambling, and poorly structured sentences.

> The ever-present danger of students resorting to thinly-disguised native language structure and lexicon when seeking to express their meaning in English cannot be ignored. Students should be sensitized to this problem which is most likely to arise when the ideas they are trying to express are complex. They should be encouraged to break down a complex idea into a series of simple affirmative statements in English which represent the facets of its meaning and then to rebuild these into complex or compound sentences which respond to the rules of combination and modification in English as they know them.

It has been suggested that the writer's first language may affect writing in English in another significant way. Kaplan (1972) has explored the possibility that writing in different cultures may differ in important ways, not least in the logical development of ideas. The implication of this is that students may need to acquire an awareness of patterns of discourse in English. Even writers of cognate languages may have difficulty in the overall organization of ideas and in the selection and development of content.

There is also the problem of words. One of my intermediate students summed it up when she described her reasons for coming to the class. One of the reasons was this:

> People tell me my English is good but they don't realize I use the same words all the time. I need more words and more ways of putting them together.

Some students need a good deal of help in developing a range of vocabulary and the ability to use it effectively. Once ideas have been generated for writing, the selection of appropriate words to communicate precise meanings, to create an effect, to develop a theme is very important. A good deal of vocabulary can be elicited or pre-taught during the pre-writing stage. As students try to express their ideas in English the teacher can provide the necessary language. But there is also room for including vocabulary-building activities in the stages of planning, writing, and rewriting, such as working with collocations or denoting attitude by using positive and negative adjectives. The tasks in this section present some ideas for this.

The question that arises from looking at the product of writing and the problems that students have in relation to various features of written discourse is this: What is the role of the teacher in helping students to produce coherent and cohesive pieces of writing? In other words:

– Can teaching help?
– Can the teacher speed up the process of writing development by presenting models for analysis?
– Is it useful for teachers, in devising tasks, to use some of the metalanguage of linguistic analysis, and raise students' awareness of how texts are put together?

The choice of tasks in this section implies a qualified 'yes' to all of these questions. The qualifications can be listed as follows:

1 Teachers who encourage their students to read in English do them a great service. It appears to be the case that good writers, who may not necessarily have had any formal instruction in discourse types, start writing with the appropriate 'schema' in their heads. They know a successful structure for a review or can make an effective plan for describing a system of some sort. This ability has built up through reading and inferring the structures of texts. So, as well as undertaking tasks to practise aspects of textual structure, students can also gain considerable insight from reading published and peer group writing.

2 Controlled tasks which focus on one or more aspects of written discourse should be balanced as a classroom activity by freer writing activities, even from the early stages. Students need to draw on their learning experience to express themselves, to exploit the language resources they have, to see what they can do, to progress towards autonomy. The tasks show a whole range of techniques, some of which guide the details of language, others of which guide content and organization, but all of which are appropriate to specific aims.

3 The most effective way of helping students to produce coherent and cohesive writing is to offer practice at the text level, that is, to encourage the writing of whole texts. Tasks which practise putting sentences together out of context are not as useful as those which take a whole text as a framework and develop practice within it. If the context of the writing is clear, all the devices in focus can be practised in a meaningful way. For this reason all the tasks presented in this section involve practice in the context of complete pieces of communication.

One final question remains to be answered. What kinds of texts do we ask our students to write? The answer to that largely depends on the reasons our students have for learning English and the purposes they have for writing English. Perhaps the first thing to note is that writing is a relatively rare activity outside the professional world, so the English language teacher needs to think carefully about the role of writing in the classroom and the demands made on students.

Several writers have proposed typologies of writing types: Davies and Widdowson (1974), Rivers and Temperley (1978), Ron White (1980), and Anita Pincas (1982). All of these make a primary distinction between personal writing and public or professional writing. This basic distinction can be further elaborated into six categories:

Personal writing is writing for oneself, and includes various kinds of aide-mémoires, as well as diaries and journals. These writing activities would normally be carried out in the first language but there may be good motivational reasons for using them in the foreign language classroom. As we have seen, keeping journals in English provides valuable practice opportunities.

Study writing is also for oneself and may never be shown to others. The student makes notes while reading, takes notes in lectures, and makes summaries for exam revision. All of these types require skills which can usefully be taught to students learning English for study purposes.

Public writing is writing as a member of the general public to organizations or institutions, so that there are certain conventions to keep to in the writing. It includes such activities as writing letters of enquiry, complaint, letters to the editor, form filling, and applications.

Creative writing can include poems, stories, rhymes, drama, all types of writing which again are mainly for oneself but which may be shared with others. It is a kind of writing most commonly found at primary and lower secondary levels in mother-tongue classrooms. In these contexts it has the values of helping personal and social development, building confidence and self-esteem, and developing writing skills through narrative. Some teachers report great success with creative writing in general-purpose English classes to adults, but careful decisions are necessary about its appropriateness and likely success with particular groups of adults.

Social writing is a category which includes all the writing that establishes and maintains social relationships with family and friends; that is, personal letters, invitations, notes with congratulations, condolences, telegrams, and telephone messages. Many of these will be relevant to EFL students who need to learn the correct formats and formulas.

Institutional writing relates to professional roles and is needed by business executives, teachers, engineers, and students in these and other fields. It may well be possible to draw up a core of this type of writing which all professional people need to be able to write, e.g. reports, summaries, minutes, memos, etc. However, each area of activity will have its own specialized texts, such as legal contracts or academic essays. Language students in these more specialized groups can usually draw up specifications of their own needs in writing English, and provide authentic products.

When designing a writing programme for a group of students, it is sensible to draw up a checklist of writing relevant to the group, or even to have an elaborated list, such as the one below, from which to draw items.

Types of writing

Personal writing	Public writing	Creative writing

diaries
journals
shopping lists
reminders for oneself
packing lists
addresses
recipes
	letters of – enquiry
	    – complaint
	    – request
	form filling
	applications (for memberships)
		poems
		stories
		rhymes
		drama
		songs
		autobiography

Social writing	**Study writing**	**Institutional writing**

letters
invitations
notes – of condolence
    – of thanks
    – of congratulations
cablegrams
telephone messages
instructions – to friends
    – to family
	making notes while reading
	taking notes from lectures
	making a card index
	summaries
	synopses
	reviews
	reports of – experiments
	    – workshops
	    – visits
	essays
	bibliographies
		agendas posters
		minutes instructions
		memoranda speeches
		reports applications
		reviews curriculum vitae
		contracts specifications
		business letters note-making
		public notices (doctors and other
		advertisements professionals)

Because of the assessment procedures which exist in many educational systems and the nature of public examinations in English language, our students usually have to develop skills in writing compositions. For some of them this will be a useful precursor to writing academic essays in English in higher education. But it is also important to ensure that students' future writing needs are met. One way to do this is to teach the core writing types, as mentioned above. Another method is to move beyond forms to functions and to organize a writing course according to various types of discourse, for example, description, discussion, narrative, etc., as these functions are present in many forms of writing.

In recent years some English language examination boards have moved towards testing students' ability to produce appropriate text types. Each writing task set in the exam needs to be organized in a particular way. If you look at the examples that follow, you will see that each requires a certain kind of functional organization.

Question 1A (10 marks)

Write a brief description of the water supply of a house. Your description should be clear and concise and is intended to accompany the simplified illustration of a house water supply in a houseowner's manual. **Start at the point where water enters the house.** Write about ten sentences in the answer book for Question 1A.

A page for rough work is provided in the answer book for Question 1A.

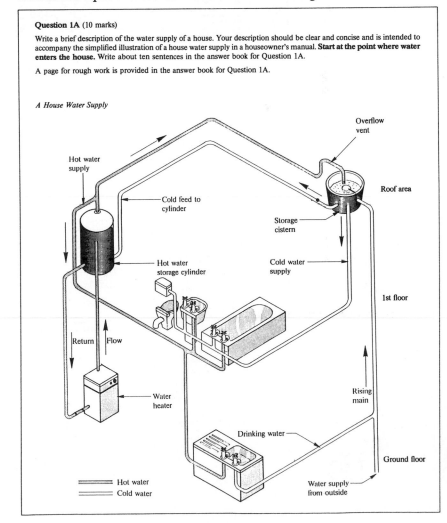

A House Water Supply

Question 1B (20 marks)

A trip to the borders

You are planning to visit Dryburgh and some of the other abbey churches in the Border Region between England and Scotland and would like to interest some other students in the trip.

Using the map provided below,

(i)   describe the route you will take from Edinburgh to Dryburgh and some of the interesting sights you will see on the journey.

Using the diagram and information on page 5,

(ii)   describe what Dryburgh Abbey was like in the past indicating what you and your friends will be able to see *now*.

Write about a page to a page and a half in total.

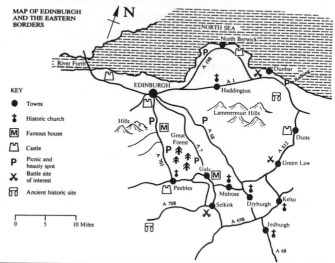

MAP OF EDINBURGH
AND THE EASTERN
BORDERS

Question 1A (10 marks)

An extractor fan is used to improve ventilation in a room. It is often placed in a kitchen to remove steam and warm air arising from cooking. To fit an extractor fan in a window it is necessary to cut a circular hole in the window pane.

Imagine that you have carried out the actions shown in the diagrams on page 3 and have to write a *report* on the work done. Write the report describing the steps followed in doing the work and use the past tense. Do *not* write instructions for doing the work.

You may, if you wish, begin your answer with the following sentence : "Diagonal lines were drawn on the window using the ruler and crayon to find the mid point".

A page for rough work is provided in the answer book for Question 1A.

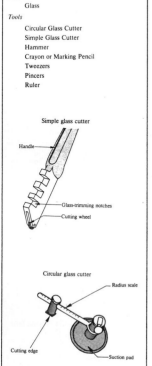

Material

     Glass

Tools

     Circular Glass Cutter
     Simple Glass Cutter
     Hammer
     Crayon or Marking Pencil
     Tweezers
     Pincers
     Ruler

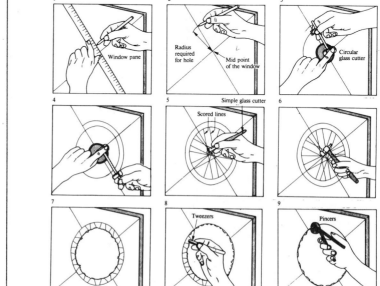

Language teachers have come to recognize a number of text types, within which the presentation of ideas follows distinctive patterns, for example, process description, instruction, discussion, etc. Clearly it is useful to make these distinctions if we want to help students to understand the different types of organization they exhibit. One particular type may form the teaching aim of a lesson, as many of the tasks in this section demonstrate. Here is a checklist of text types which was drawn up to cover the English needs of a group of students following a range of courses in the first year of college. Each week of the course focused on one type.

Types of writing	Purpose
Static description	describing a place, system, etc.
Process description	describing the sequence of steps in how something is done or the operations in how something works
Narrative	telling a sequence of events in a report or biography
Cause and effect	explaining how events are linked, how one thing leads to another, giving reasons for outcomes
Discussion	putting forward arguments, evidence, examples, etc.
Comparison	comparing and contrasting
Classification	organizing a description into a hierarchy of categories
Definition	defining, explaining, and exemplifying something

A similar approach was taken recently in designing the writing programme within a course in which students were preparing for the Cambridge Certificate of Proficiency in English. An analysis of past papers and practice tasks in published learning materials showed that titles fell within the same list of text types.

Comparison and Contrast	What are the advantages of the extended family system? 'The countryside has all that is good in life, the city all that is bad.' Discuss.
Discussion	'Today's luxuries are tomorrow's necessities.' Discuss. 'Conversation is a lost art.' Discuss. 'Crime is on the increase in cities.' How can it be controlled?
Narrative	Describe an historical event at which you would like to have been present.
Cause/effect	Discuss the causes of violence in the modern world. What features in their home life might assist in moulding antisocial young people? Discuss the effects of pollution on the sea. What effect do strikes have on the economy of a country?
Definition	Define 'stress' and discuss its causes and remedies. What do you understand by the term 'freedom of speech'? What do you think should be its limitations?
Static Description	Describe and discuss the provisions made for nursery education in your country. Give an account of a famous person who has significantly influenced society.
Review	Suggest three books of contrasting types which you would enjoy rereading and justify your high opinion of each.

The issue remains as to how to integrate the teaching of various skills required for successful crafting. One suggestion is to work out a programme of tasks, specifying function, form, focus, and context. An early task in such a programme could be:

Function	Form	Focus	Context
Dynamic description of a scene	Extract from a letter: one paragraph	Selection of content: topic, focus, logical development of ideas	Describing the scene around you as you write a letter home

a later task might be

Narrative	A letter reporting a family event	Paragraphing	Reporting the sequence of events at a family wedding

and later

Comparison	A letter	Cohesive devices used for comparison and contrast	Advising a friend on the better of two holiday alternatives

Contexts are not always easy to create, especially for school students whose future needs in English are unpredictable. And sometimes it is advisable to set writing tasks in preparation for an examination in which contexts are not necessarily given and where students need to create their own.

Rivers and Temperley (1978) provide a useful idea for planning a series of writing tasks in context. Their solution is to create global contexts within the class by creating a country or a family. Students can prepare different types of writing, descriptions, biographies, reports, discussions, and newspaper articles for the file on the Fielding family or the portfolio on the province of Pomerania. In this way the students invent their own imaginary setting. This generates ideas for many different writing tasks and provides a realistic context for them.

The tasks on the following pages are specified by function, form, focus, and context. There is a wide variety of activities. The focus of some is more on reading as a preliminary to writing. They show how various types of textual analysis can help the writer to appreciate what makes a successful product in terms of linking ideas within or across sentences or in terms of the overall organization of the discourse. Other tasks involve students in substantial pieces of writing and practise the use of connectives, how to develop a sequence of ideas through a paragraph, or how to organize discourse according to its function, whether description, narrative, discussion, contrast, cause and effect, etc. The emphasis throughout is on these types of discourse, required by students in study or institutional writing and in writing for school examinations – still one of the major reasons for writing in English at the school level. Other types of writing, such as personal or business letters are very adequately dealt with in a variety of general and supplementary coursebooks.

3.1 Organizing a non-chronological description

This type of description is not normally a complete text type. It usually forms a part of another text type. For example, it is often found in personal writing such as letters and journals when the writer wants to capture what is happening around him or her. The task below takes the context of writing a letter home and wanting to capture present experiences for the reader by describing the environment in a dynamic way (and thereby using progressive forms).

LEVEL	**Intermediate**
TOPIC	**A scene as a moment in time**
FUNCTION	Dynamic description.
FORM	Personal letter.
FOCUS	Discourse organization in non-chronological description.
CONTEXT	The students are staying with families in England. At the moment they are writing letters to friends at home, and they want to give a taste of their present life, surroundings, and experiences by describing the scene around them and what is happening in it. Overleaf is a picture of the kind of setting they might describe.
PREPARATION	There are several ways of preparing for this task:

1 You can make a collection of cut-out magazine pictures of appropriate scenes, such as:
  – the family in the garden on a summer afternoon
  – the scene around you in a park or playground
  – a picnic in the countryside
  – on the beach
  – an event, e.g. a fête, a rally.

2 Alternatively, you can introduce the task in a previous lesson and ask the students to find their own picture.

3 You also need to have a larger picture which the whole class can see.

IN CLASS

1 Explain first the context of the writing, using the large picture, eliciting ideas from the class about what to comment on. As they make suggestions, show them by grouping suggestions on the blackboard, what in general might go into the description:
– where things are in relation to each other
– what can be seen, heard, felt, smelt, etc.
– details about key people and things
– what is happening at the moment

2 Ask the students to work in pairs and ask each pair to work on one picture. To begin with, each partner in the pair should work individually on a first draft, describing the scene as if they were sitting somewhere in the picture.

3 While the students are working, monitor them and give help where necessary. Then, while they are finishing, write a set of questions on the blackboard:
– *What does the writer describe first? And last?*
– *Why do you think he/she has followed that order?*
– *Do you think the writer has begun with the most important thing?*
– *Which adjectives has the writer used?*
– *Has the writer focused on one or more of the senses of sight, sound, taste, smell, etc?*
– *What do you think is the best part of the description?*
– *Has the writer left out anything you wrote about in your own description?*
– *Has the writer included anything which you missed out?*

4 Ask students to exchange their writing. They should examine each other's work in the light of the questions on the blackboard.

5 Students can then discuss the similarities and differences in their approach and suggest improvements to each other before redrafting their own composition.

3.2 Using connectors of addition

This task attempts to demonstrate the point made in the introduction to this section that, as students learn conjunctions in English, they need to be aware of their grammatical restrictions. I have deliberately taken addition as the function. Many teachers think this is a relatively easy area but experience shows that students have problems with the positions of 'also' and 'as well as'.

LEVEL

Lower intermediate upwards

TOPIC

Leisure activities

FUNCTION

Describing habits and customs.

FORM

An information brochure.

FOCUS

Using connectors of addition.

CONTEXT

The students are writing an information brochure for immigrants or guest workers or visitors to their country. The topic is leisure and state support for leisure.

PREPARATION

You need to make copies of the text overleaf and of the task sheet which shows the grammatical constraints on the connectives of addition.

IN CLASS

1 Ask students to work in pairs. Write a few questions on the blackboard for them to ask each other:
– *What are the most popular leisure-time activities in your country?*
– *What are the national sports?*
– *What other outdoor recreations are popular?*
– *What help does the State give in providing leisure facilities?*

2 Ask some of the students to report back their findings. Use the reporting session to expand vocabulary.

3 Ask students to read the text and to underline all the examples of words and phrases which add one idea to another.

4 Ask students to study the table and to write down five things about leisure time in their own country. They should try to use a different word or phrase from the table each time. As they do this, circulate and help, watching for any particular problems which may need further explanation and practice.

5 Ask students to exchange their writing and try to correct each other's work.

6 They are now ready to take their first draft and produce a more detailed piece of writing about leisure time in their own country.

TEXT

Read this short text about leisure time in Sweden. It is taken from a guide to immigrants and guest workers in Sweden. Study how the connectors of addition are used.

The Swedish people spend a great deal of their leisure time at home but they are *also* very regular cinema, theatre, and concert goers. A lot of people belong to clubs *and* some attend study circles *too*. Sports and outdoor recreations are popular: walking, swimming, fishing, boating, skiing, and skating *as well as* home-centred activities such as gardening.

The state and local authorities provide active support for leisure by subsidizing youth clubs, community centres, and other cultural organizations. *In addition*, most communities are provided with public libraries where people can borrow books, films, records, and tapes.

TASK SHEET

Make sure you know how these words can link ideas. The table below shows their usual position in the sentence.

as well as	can go in the middle of a sentence as above or can go at the beginning. If it precedes a verb the gerund is used: – *As well as* swimming, the Swedes like many other water sports.
too	goes at the end of a sentence or clause
In addition	usually goes at the beginning of a sentence and is followed by a comma
also	normally comes mid-sentence, and is placed after the verb *to be* or an auxiliary verb or before a main verb: – They *also* stole four watches. – The driver has *also* been arrested. – He is *also* the best student.
and	with two co-ordinate clauses, addition can simply be indicated by using *and*.

Imagine you are writing a similar guide for visitors to your own country. Write two paragraphs about leisure and try to use the connectors of addition shown above.

3.3 Using cohesive devices

LEVEL

Intermediate

TOPIC

A school guide

FUNCTION

Describing a place.

FORM

A visitor's guide or publicity brochure.

FOCUS

Combining ideas using a range of cohesive devices and a range of sentence patterns.

CONTEXT

The students are designing a visitor's guide to their school, college, or the language school in which they are studying.

PREPARATION

Students should each have a copy of the task sheet overleaf. This serves as an example. You can base the same kind of activity on a variety of texts by breaking down the text into fairly simple sentences.

For this particular topic it would also be useful to have examples of brochures for students to skim through.

IN CLASS

1 Put students into groups and ask them to think of the things they would include in an information brochure about the institution. They may like to skim through any brochures you have made available. Ask them to make a list of all of the points.

2 Take suggestions from the class and write up a set of points on the blackboard which students can add to their lists:

- situation
- history
- buildings
- equipment and facilities
- types of students
- subjects

3 Then ask students individually to make notes on their own choice of institution, selecting the most relevant categories.

4 Give out copies of the task sheet and go through it with the class, taking suggestions on how to combine the sentences and writing the end product up on the blackboard.

5 Encourage students to think carefully about how to combine ideas as they use their notes to write their own descriptions.

REMARKS

My own experience is that this kind of task, combining sentences by using logical connectives or by creating co-ordinating clauses, is useful for some students but not for others. It depends partly on whether they have received any training in grammatical description. Teachers of multilingual classes with students from a range of educational backgrounds may find that this is true of only some of their students. My own procedure is to do one task of this nature with the class and then prepare others as an extra resource which students can choose to do at home or in study periods for individual marking.

TASK SHEET

Combine the sentences below to make a text by following the instructions given.

1 Belvedere College is a multi-million-dollar institution.

2 It is a few kilometres from the centre of the Zimbabwean capital, Harare.

3 The training college spreads over 26 hectares of grounds.

Combine sentences 1, 2, and 3
Begin with:
  Spreading across . . .

4 The US Agency for International Development granted 12 million dollars for the project.

5 Local contractors began construction in June 1982.

Combine sentences 4 and 5.
Begin with:
  After . . .

6 Students at Belvedere are required to take two subjects.

7 One must be technical and the other must be non-technical.

Combine sentences 6 and 7 by using a comma and reducing sentence 7.

8 The college is equipped with a modern cafeteria, lecture halls, and seminar rooms.

9 It has workshops, a gymnasium, and a swimming pool.

Use a connective of addition to combine sentences 8 and 9.

3.4 Analysing the reference system of a text

This exercise concentrates specifically on reference as a cohesive device. The purpose is to draw the students' attention explicitly to this cohesive device so that they can appreciate how to use it, and what sorts of words and phrases can be used.

LEVEL **Intermediate**

TOPIC **The Eskimos**

FUNCTION Historical description.

FORM Biographical account of a group of people, such as might be found in an information guide or review.

FOCUS Creating a reference system in a text.

PREPARATION 1 You need to make copies of both texts shown overleaf.

2 Alternatively, the first text can be copied onto the blackboard or shown on an OHP.

IN CLASS 1 Begin by asking the class what they know about the Eskimo people. Elicit as much information as you can, writing any new words on the blackboard and checking that the whole class understands them.

2 Show the students the passage you have copied onto the transparency. Ask them to read it through quickly. Put a ring round the first reference item *They* and ask the class to tell you what it refers to earlier in the text.

3 Then put rings around the other reference items and ask students to do the same exercise with those.

4 Check through all the answers with the class.

5 Give out the second text and ask students to work quietly writing the nouns or phrases and the substitute words in the right column. Encourage them to check with each other while working.

6 Ask students at home to find information of a similar nature about a group of people in their own country and to write two or three paragraphs.

7 When the students bring their completed writing into class, ask them to exchange their work with a partner. The partner should carry out a similar task of ringing the pronouns, adjectives, etc. and linking them back to earlier items in the passage. Encourage students to discuss their work and see what improvements can be made.

TEXT A

Look at the way these ideas are linked in the text:

> The Eskimos are descendants of hunters who
> moved from Siberia into Northern Canada at the
> end of the last Ice Age, about 12,000 years ago.
> They still live in this area where there are
> arctic weather conditions for eight or nine
> months of the year. In such a climate it is not
> possible to develop agriculture. The
> traditional Eskimo economy was therefore based
> on two basic activities. The first was fishing
> through holes in the ice or on the open water in
> canoes. The second was hunting of sea mammals
> such as whales and seals, and of land mammals
> such as caribou.

Now find examples of similar links in the paragraph below. Write the pronoun or adjective or other substitute word in the second column and the noun or phrase which it substitutes for in the first column.

TEXT B

Until about 1960 the Eskimos lived a traditional life, grouped in small communities, each one containing about fifty people. Their homes were snowhouses and tents, the latter made from caribou skins. They traded furs with local trading companies to obtain equipment like strong wooden sledges.

In the 1960s the Canadian government took an interest in the Eskimos. It loaned money for fish-freezing plants and fishing boats. This was intended to develop and strengthen the economy. It also provided schools and health clinics. These were staffed by government teachers and nurses. Unfortunately, modernization has brought social problems too. The most serious of these is alcohol abuse.

nouns or phrases	substitute word(s)
e.g. The Eskimos	*their*

3.5 Organizing general and supporting statements

In this activity students create a text from isolated sentences. In doing so, their attention is drawn to one way of organizing the information in a text. The text below consists of four paragraphs, each of which is composed of a topic sentence and some supporting sentences. The topic sentence is a generalization and the supporting sentences are more specific or are examples. In putting the pieces of the text together students begin to appreciate the structure of discourse and how they can develop ideas through a piece of writing.

LEVEL

Advanced

TOPIC

Stress

FUNCTION

Definition.

FORM

A formal scientific text as found in a textbook or academic essay.

FOCUS

Understanding how paragraphs can organize information.

PREPARATION

You need to prepare copies of the task sheet.

IN CLASS

1 A useful warm-up to the topic knowledge in the text is to ask students to work in pairs and answer the following questions:

a. *Can you think of an example of someone who is suffering from stress?*
b. *Is stress always harmful?*
c. *Have you ever suffered from stress? Looking back, can you understand why?*

2 Hold a short feedback session to see what students can report.

3 Give out the task sheet and explain it very clearly to the students.

4 Ask students first to find the four general statements and to write them under the letters a, b, c, and d.

5 It is useful to check at this point, so that everyone starts the second part of the task with the correct information.

6 Then ask students to find the supporting statements. Encourage them to check with each other as they are working.

7 When you have checked the answers, ask students to work in pairs and decide on the best order of paragraphs.

8 Finally, when you have checked this and asked them to give reasons for this order, see if they can suggest a title for the completed passage.

TASK SHEET

In the twelve sentences below you will find four general statements and eight more specific supporting statements or examples. First find the four general statements and write the numbers of the sentences at the top of each column.

	a	b	c	d
general statements	. . . . . .	. . . . . .	. . . . . .	. . . . . .
supporting statements	. . . . . .	. . . . . .	. . . . . .	. . . . . .
	. . . . . .	. . . . . .	. . . . . .	. . . . . .

Now find the two supporting statements or examples which 'belong' to each general statement and write the numbers of those sentences in the correct column.

1 Others bother us continually and make us feel under stress.

2 Predicting stress is quite a problem.

3 Alternatively, a young woman may find herself becoming increasingly bored, impatient, and irritable in a trivial office job.

4 There is a key difference between healthy and harmful stress.

5 Many of these adjustments take place without our being conscious of them.

6 It is easy to look back on an experience, knowing it has done harm and to say that it was stress that caused it.

7 Our lives are full of change and we continually try to adjust as well as possible to all the changes going on about us.

8 In healthy stress there is a rapid adjustment to the change.

9 Stress can best be described as the reaction of the mind and the body to change.

10 It is only those changes which we have no answer to and cannot adjust to which cause physical and mental suffering.

11 For example, a man who takes up a job as a long distance lorry driver may find that his body reacts badly to irregular meals, and develops a duodenal ulcer.

12 It is not so easy to predict in advance that we will be harmed by going through a particular experience.

You now have the content of four paragraphs. Decide on the most sensible order of paragraphs and give the passage a title.

NOTE: *You may make photocopies of this for classroom use (but please note that copyright law does not normally permit multiple copying of published material).*

3.6 Transferring information to a diagram

The following task uses the well established technique of information transfer, in this case transferring information from a prose text to a diagram which represents the information content of the text. It is a particularly useful technique with texts that have the major function of classifying, as it is relatively easy to devise a diagram which indicates criteria for classification, resulting groups, and examples within those groups. It is a reading task which helps students to see how such a text is organized, and provides them with an understanding of discourse structure which will enable them to write their own classifications appropriately.

LEVEL

Upper intermediate

TOPIC

Taking vitamins

FUNCTION

Classification.

FORM

A formal scientific description as found in a textbook or academic essay.

FOCUS

Developing understanding of discourse organization.

PREPARATION

You can use any text which contains a classification of this type appropriate to the level of the students. You will need copies of the text, one for each student in the class. The diagram (Figure 9) can be copied or drawn on the blackboard.

IN CLASS

1 A useful warm-up to the topic knowledge contained in the text is to ask students if any of them take vitamins and to say why (or to say why they do not think it is necessary). Then ask them what types of people may take extra vitamins. This can be undertaken as classwork with you asking questions and eliciting information, or as pair work with the following questions written on the blackboard:

– *Do you take vitamins? Why or why not?*
– *What sorts of people need to take vitamins?*

2 If this is the first time that your students have done this kind of information transfer activity, ask them to skim through the text and to decide what sort of text it is, that is, discussion, classification, contrast, or comparison.

3 Give out the diagram and ask the students to find the information they need to fill in the two blank boxes beside 'level of potency of vitamin supplementation'. Check with the whole class after a minute.

4 Then ask students to work quietly and find the information they need to complete the diagram. Encourage them to check with each other as they work.

TEXT

Read the text and complete Figure 9 below:

Taking vitamins
This is a controversial subject for both ordinary people and the medical profession. Do we need vitamin supplements and if so, why? To what extent do we take them? We can divide vitamin supplementation into three simple categories, each of which needs a different level of potency.

We know that modern food processing reduces vitamin content and over-cooking reduces it still further. Anyone who eats a lot of processed food may suffer from vitamin deficiency and need to take supplements. So, too, may elderly people who do not have a proper diet. There are also some sections of the population which have lower social and economic status and may not be able to afford a good diet. All of these people may benefit from a general, all-round supplementation of vitamins to ensure the minimum daily requirement.

The second category of vitamin supplementation may be needed by people whose life-styles increase their need for certain vitamins. For example, people who work under stressful conditions may need more vitamin B. The habits of smoking and drinking rob the body of certain vitamins. Such cases may need up to five times the recommended daily intake. In addition, many medicinal drugs can reduce absorption of vitamins or cause them to be excreted in abnormal quantities, for example, antibiotics, aspirin, and the contraceptive pill.

The third category of supplementation is administration of doses of 10–100 times the recommended amount. This is called the 'therapeutic' use of vitamins and it is a matter of great controversy. It does appear to be the case, however, that complaints such as heart and blood diseases, respiratory infections, and skin complaints all benefit from large intakes of certain vitamins.

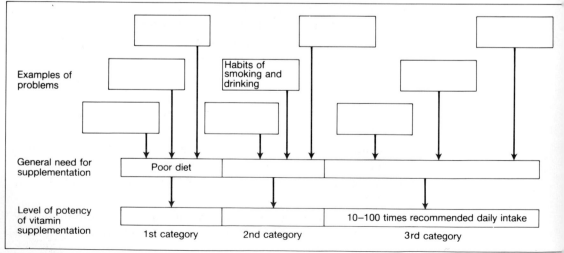

Figure 9

3.7 Unscrambling a text

In this activity the text has been separated out into its component sentences which have been arranged in random order. The task for students is to re-create the text by deciding on the correct order. Some words and phrases have been underlined to draw attention to their role in linking the parts of the original text. The task is essentially a reading task but is a very useful preliminary to writing, as it shows students the devices used to join ideas in discourse.

LEVEL   **Elementary to intermediate**

TOPIC   **A robbery**

FUNCTION   Reporting an incident.

FORM   A newspaper article.

FOCUS   Understanding how cohesive devices work in a text.

PREPARATION   There are two alternatives for this task:

a. Either the task sheet can be copied from the blackboard, and students encouraged to write the correct order of sentences in the boxes.
b. Or you can make enough copies of the exercise for the class to work in pairs. Cut up each text into strips, with one sentence on each strip, and place them in envelopes.

IN CLASS   1 Explain to students that they are going to read a newspaper article about a robbery, but first they have to create the article from a set of sentences.

2 Give out one envelope to each pair of students and ask them to set out the sentences on the desk top.

3 Each pair is to put the sentences in the correct order.

4 When they have finished, they should try to explain to each other how the underlined words and phrases helped them.

5 Encourage them to check across with other pairs.

6 Ask them to make up a headline for the article.

TASK SHEET

The following sentences can be put together to form a newspaper report but they are in the wrong order. Work with a partner. Put them in the right order and decide how the words and phrases underlined help to link the parts of the text. Then compare your answer with those of other pairs.

☐ They had followed him into a multi-storey car park where he had left his car while attending an evening course.

☐ They made off with £50 in cash, leaving the driver bruised and cut.

☐ A man was beaten and robbed by two thugs in Bond Street on Wednesday evening.

☐ The victim, from Wembley, had just sat in the driving seat when two men wrenched open the door, pulled him to the ground, punched him, and stole his wallet.

☐ One was wearing a gold chain around his neck.

☐ Anyone with information should contact their local police station.

☐ The attackers were both between 18 and 20, of medium height, and were wearing dark sunglasses and dark leather jackets.

☐ The other had three gold ear-rings in his left ear.

Write the correct order (1, 2, 3, etc.) in the boxes.

NOTE: You may make photocopies of this for classroom use (but please note that copyright law does not normally permit multiple copying of published material).

3.8 Writing a newspaper article

LEVEL

Lower intermediate upwards (This could also be used with elementary students if the newspaper article were chosen with care.

TOPIC

Villages threatened by rodents

FUNCTION

Reporting an event.

FORM

A report as found in a newspaper article.

FOCUS

Overall organization and development of ideas.

PREPARATION

You need to find two newspaper articles reporting the same incident but each containing slightly different information. Alternatively, one longer article may be divided so that each part contains different information.

You also need to prepare a set of questions about the reported incident

1 Ask the students to work in pairs. Give each student in the pair the set of questions and one of the articles. The following are examples of the type of questions to prepare:

– *Where have the hordes of mice appeared?*
– *Which area are they moving towards?*
– *When did they first appear?*
– *What do they look like?*
– *Which species of rodent could they be?*
– *What do they eat?*
– *What actions have farmers taken against them?*
– *Were these actions successful?*
– *Why are the farmers and villagers so worried?*

2 Allow time for the students to read their articles, find answers to the questions, and make notes.

3 Students should then work in pairs, asking each other the questions and pooling information, making notes as they do so. Sometimes only one student will have relevant information and sometimes both of them will have points to contribute.

4 When the students have completed exchanging information and making notes, they are ready to draft their own article. You can help them with paragraphing by suggesting sub-headings to be followed:

– Millions of Rodents
– Mystery Identity
– Terrified Cats Fled
– Villages Threatened

Try to encourage students to work from their notes and use their own language resources as much as possible to write the article. However, even if students incorporate a good many expressions from the originals, this can be beneficial to their development of written English.

Poison Fails to Halt Mice Hordes

From our correspondent BELGRADE Tuesday

Millions of mice advancing across Bosnia into Serbia have become immune to poison put down to halt their march, it was reported today.

Farmers said they had seen the mice swallow the poison and then continue to attack crops without any apparent ill effects. Crops in ten villages in Bosnia have been destroyed.

The rodents, six inches long with yellow coats, are eating up wheat, rye, barley, rice, potatoes, and white beans. They are even climbing trees.

Our nature correspondent tells us that rodents which are six inches long are unlikely to be house mice or common rats. The horde could be made up of hamsters, forest doormice, wood mice or yellownecks, all of which are found in Eastern Europe.

As for their so-called immunity to poison, it is not uncommon for rodents to creep away out of sight when they have been poisoned. It may be that they disappear into holes and crevices.

Villages threatened by rodents

Millions of Rodents

Millions of mice are plaguing the villages of Bosnia and are moving across into Serbia.

The hordes, which first appeared a month ago in the region, have multiplied and spread out in ever-increasing numbers across the countryside. They are now threatening several villages near the Serbian town of Priboi na Limu.

CATS FLED IN TERROR

Experts first believed that the mice would turn on each other once they had eaten all the available food in the fields. But the mice have moved on to new areas. They are reported to be so thick on the ground now that 10-15 of them can be counted to every square yard. They are plaguing the farmyards as well as the fields. Scores of cats set on them fled in terror.

PANIC - STRICKEN VILLAGERS

Panic-stricken villagers have appealed to the authorities for help. One group said: "We will be left not only without food but we will be swallowed up ourselves."

3.9 Sequencing ideas in a story

LEVEL

Elementary upwards (depending on the story you choose). The story chosen here can be used with lower intermediate students, as the vocabulary work is appropriate to that level.

TOPIC

A mystery story

FUNCTION

Narrating a story.

FORM

Composition.

FOCUS

Overall organization and logical sequencing of ideas.

CONTEXT

Creative writing which may be useful preparation for narratives set in examinations.

PREPARATION

1 You need to find a short mystery story or to make one up. The text given at the end of task 3.9 was written by a fourteen-year-old British secondary school pupil and the activity has worked well with teenage pupils (as well as adults). Formulate a set of questions about the story which are in chronological order and which suit the level of your learners. These can be written on the blackboard or copied for the students. Alternatively, it is possible to imagine the framework of a story and to make up questions accordingly.

2 You also need to work out a list of vocabulary items for the activity at step 2. These items could be put on the blackboard or copies made for pair work.

IN CLASS

1 Tell your students that you are going to read the opening of a story. You want them to listen and tell you what kind of story it is. Read the

text up to the sentence which ends with 'anxious'. Elicit that it could be a mystery, ghost, or horror story and ask them how they could tell.

2 Remind them that adjectives are important for atmosphere. Give them a list of adjectives which can be used to describe a house. Ask them to work in pairs, use a dictionary, and talk to each other in order to complete the chart.

Adjective	What does it mean?	Is it positive or negative?
gloomy cosy welcoming draughty dismal cheerful		

3 Tell your students that they are going to write a story through following a framework of questions which you have devised. Make it clear that the questions serve only as a guide and allow for quite a degree of flexibility. Different students may end up with quite different stories. The story outlined by the questions is incomplete so students can make up their own endings.

4 Give out the questions or write them on the blackboard and ask students to write a passage on which the questions could be based. They should treat the questions as a flexible framework within which to make up the opening episodes of a story. For example:

- *Why was Susan staying with Catherine's family in Wales?*
- *Why did she feel unhappy and nervous when she went to her room on the first night?*
- *What was unfamiliar about night in the country?*
- *Why did she wake up during the night?*
- *What did she do first when she woke up?*
- *Why did she get out of bed?*
- *What did she discover at the window?*
- *How did she know there was a cat in the room?*
- *How could she tell it had jumped on the bed?*
- *What happened when she reached out to stroke it?*

5 An optional stage is to let students work in pairs or groups to discuss a possible story and make notes which individuals can then use in their own stories.

6 Give students time to complete their individual narratives. Then ask them to exchange stories with each other and to compare efforts.

7 If you have based the questions on a real story, read it dramatically to the class before asking students to complete their narratives for homework.

TEXT

I was going to stay for some weeks with my friend Catherine's family in a small Welsh village. It was the school holidays and my parents had gone to my grandfather's funeral far away in Africa. I was fourteen years old.

The first night there, my bedroom was cold and unwelcoming. I felt unhappy and anxious. I wasn't used to the country and the quiet night outside. There was no familiar street lamp shining through my window and no busy traffic noise outside.

I hurried into bed and hid under the blankets, only my eyes and the tip of my nose outside the covers. The voices of the grown-ups downstairs buzzed quietly below but I fell asleep almost at once.

Sometime in the night I started suddenly awake. I lay still for a moment wondering what had woken me. The room was black. No light showed anywhere. And then a tapping came at the window. Tap . . . tap . . ., a soft stealthy sound. I got out of bed, trembling with cold and fear. My heart was beating loudly as I moved towards the window. My fingers twitched aside the corner of the curtain and my heart leapt into my mouth as I saw a dark shape against the window. But it was only the branch of a tree. Hurriedly, I ran back to the warmth of my bed and lay shivering under the covers.

It was then that I heard the sound of a cat, purring quietly in the room. I like cats. Catherine's family had several. I began to relax as the purring got louder and the cat came across to find me. It jumped on the bed and I felt it settling against my legs. Feeling much safer, I reached out my hand to stroke it. My fingers moved over the place where I felt its weight, but they found nothing. There was no cat there . . .

I felt that terrible nightmare feeling rush over me again.

3.10 Combining narrative and direct speech

Narratives are often recommended for writing because the organization of ideas is easier than in other types of discourse. The narrative follows a chronological sequence. It is therefore a useful way of encouraging students, especially at school, who need to practise writing. The task is made easier if there is content to hand, such as a local legend or folk-tale for the narrative.

LEVEL   **Intermediate upwards**

TOPIC   **A folk-tale or legend**

FUNCTION   Fictional narrative (based on a folk-tale or legend).

FORM	Narrative.
CONTEXT	Not many students will need to write whole narratives in a foreign language except for examination purposes. This task is for them and for those who enjoy creative writing.
FOCUS	Direct speech in narrative.
PREPARATION	1 You need to find a folk-tale or legend like the one overleaf, which can be read dramatically or, even better, which can be retold to the students.
	2 Copy out one section of the folk-tale containing direct speech as an extract to show the rules of direct speech.

IN CLASS

1 Begin by giving a dramatic reading or retelling of the legend.

2 Elicit parts of the story again from the students by asking questions so that together the class recreates the story.
  - *What time of year was it?*
  - *Why was the farmer riding to market?*
  - *Why did the mare refuse to go on?*

3 On the blackboard, write some words which represent typical themes in folk-tales or legends (*greed, patriotism, honour, duty, love, adventure, mercy, magic, fortune*), and ask students which of these relate to this story. Have a short class discussion.

4 Remind students that the story you told contained some direct speech. Ask them to look at the extract below, and go through the questions and rules with them.

5 Ask each student to think of a legend which relates to one of the themes you discussed earlier and to write it as a narrative with direct speech.

6 The stories should be published in some form.

EXTRACT

Rules for direct speech
There are rules for setting out direct speech in a story. Look at the extracts below and overleaf and see if you can discover them.

> Near Thieves' Hole the mare stopped: the stranger was there. Thinking any price now better than none, the farmer agreed to sell.
>   'How much will you give?' he said.
>   'Enough. Now come with me.'
> By Seven Firs and Goldenstone they went, to Stormy Point and Saddlebole.
>
> 1 How can you tell which words are actually spoken?
> 2 How does the writer keep the speech apart from the story?
> 3 Where does the question mark go when there is a question in direct speech?
> 4 Is there a capital letter after the question mark?
> 5 Why does the writer start lines in from the margin?
> 6 Why does he start one new line after another?

a. Put the words which are actually spoken inside inverted commas.

b. Separate the spoken words from the reporting words, *he said*, by a punctuation mark, e.g. a comma, or a question mark.

c. Include this punctuation mark inside the inverted commas. In English the inverted commas at the beginning and end of the speech are at the same level, just above the letters.

d. Whenever there is a change of speaker, start the speech on a new line a little way in from the margin.

NOTE: You may make photocopies of this for classroom use (but please note that copyright law does not normally permit multiple copying of published material).

TEXT

The Legend of Alderley

At dawn one still October day in the long ago of the world, across the hill of Alderley, a farmer from Mobberley was riding to Macclesfield fair.

The morning was dull, but mild; light mists bedimmed his way; the woods were hushed; the day promised fine. The farmer was in good spirits, and he let his horse, a milk-white mare, set her own pace, for he wanted her to arrive fresh for the market. A rich man would walk back to Mobberley that night.

So, his mind in the town while he was yet on the hill, the farmer drew near to the place known as Thieves' Hole. And there the horse stood still and would answer to neither spur nor rein. The spur and rein she understood, and her master's stern command, but the eyes that held her were stronger than all of these.

In the middle of the path, where surely there had been no one, was an old man, tall, with long hair and beard. 'You go to sell this mare,' he said. 'I come here to buy. What is your price?'

But the farmer wished to sell only at the market, where he would have the choice of many offers, so he rudely bade the stranger quit the path and let him through, for if he stayed longer he would be late to the fair.

'Then go your way,' said the old man. 'None will buy. And I shall await you here at sunset.'

The next moment he was gone, and the farmer could not tell how or where.

The day was warm, and the tavern cool, and all who saw the mare agreed that she was a splendid animal, the pride of Cheshire, a queen among horses; and everyone said that there was no finer beast in the town. But no one offered to buy. A sour-eyed farmer rode out of Macclesfield at the end of the day.

Near Thieves' Hole the mare stopped: the stranger was there.

Thinking any price now better than none, the farmer agreed to sell. 'How much will you give?' he said.

'Enough. Now come with me.'

By Seven Firs and Goldenstone they went, to Stormy Point and Saddlebole. And they halted before a great rock embedded in the hill-side. The old man lifted his staff and lightly touched the rock, and it split with the noise of thunder.

At this, the farmer toppled from his plunging horse and, on his knees, begged the other to have mercy on him and let him go his way unharmed. The horse should stay; he did not want her. Only spare his life, that was enough.

The wizard, for such he was, commanded the farmer to rise. 'I promise you safe conduct,' he said. 'Do not be afraid; for living wonders you shall see here.'

Beyond the rock stood a pair of iron gates. These the wizard opened, and took the farmer and his horse down a narrow tunnel deep into the hill. A light, subdued but beautiful, marked their way. The passage ended, and they stepped into a cave, and there a wondrous sight met the farmer's eyes – a hundred and forty knights in silver armour, and by the side of all but one a milk-white mare.

'Here they lie in enchanted sleep,' said the wizard, 'until a day will come – and come it will – when England shall be in direst peril, and England's mothers weep. Then out from the hill these must ride and, in a battle thrice lost, thrice won, upon the plain, drive the enemy into the sea.'

The farmer, dumb with awe, turned with the wizard into a further cavern, and here mounds of gold and silver and precious stones lay strewn along the ground.

'Take what you can carry in payment for the horse.'

And when the farmer had crammed his pockets (ample as his lands!), his shirt, and his fists with jewels, the wizard hurried him up the long tunnel and thrust him out of the gates. The farmer stumbled, the thunder rolled, he looked, and there was only the rock above him. He was alone on the hill, near Stormy Point. The broad full moon was up, and it was night.

And although in later years he tried to find the place, neither he nor any after him ever saw the iron gates again.

3.11 Time sequencing in a narrative

LEVEL   Intermediate

TOPIC   **A cartoon adventure**

FUNCTION   Describing and reporting events in a fictional narrative.

FORM   Fictional narrative.

FOCUS   Time adverbials and phrases to show time sequences.

PREPARATION   You need to make copies of the cartoon story on the next page.

IN CLASS   1 Point out to your students the conventions of a cartoon story, namely:

a. the caption at the top of a picture, which usually says something about the time sequence;

b. the bubble with round lines which is a speech bubble;

c. the bubble with wavy lines which is a thought bubble (as in pictures 9 and 10).

2 Ask students to skim through the story individually in order to get an impression of the time sequence and then ask them to match the following captions with pictures 2–8.

A little while later . . .

During the afternoon . . .

As the farm came in sight . . .

Later, that evening . . .

Suddenly, as they followed a bend in the river . . .

As evening darkened into night . . .

Before going outside to investigate . . .

3 Ask students to work in pairs. First ask them to check each other's captions and then ask them to make up captions for the last two pictures.

4 Still working in pairs, the students should make up the speech for each frame of the story.

5 Ask them to decide if the story ends here on a note of suspense, or if they wish to add any more. What endings are possible?

6 Discuss the endings with the class.

7 Ask students individually to write the story, paying attention to the time sequence, and ask them to make up their own titles depending on their choice of ending.

CARTOON STORY

3.12 Selecting and categorizing content

LEVEL

Intermediate upwards

TOPIC

A biography

FUNCTION

Giving biographical information.

FORM

Narrative.

FOCUS

Selecting and organizing content for a biography; denoting attitude through choice of positive and negative adjectives.

CONTEXT

Making a class magazine containing biographies of famous men and women from the students' own country or, in the case of multilingual classes, from around the world.

PREPARATION

1 Make copies of a task sheet like the one shown overleaf for individual students.

2 Or make enough copies of your task sheet for students to work in pairs, and cut up the headings and questions so that each one is on a separate piece of paper. These should then be put into envelopes. If the information is copied onto pieces of thicker card these will make a resource which can be repeatedly used with different classes.

3 Make copies of the quotations about Ghandi, with possible adjectives by the side.

IN CLASS

1 Start the activity by writing the word 'Biography' on the blackboard and asking students to explain what it means. Then ask if anyone has read a biography recently or show them one or tell them about one you have read.

2 Introduce the idea of what might go into a biography by writing 'Birthplace' on the blackboard. Ask students what else they would expect to find in a biography and add some other headings.

3 Give out the envelopes and ask the students to work in pairs. Each pair should try to match the headings and questions in their envelope.

4 Ask students if they want to add any other headings.

5 Discuss with the class whether or not there is a logical order.

6 Ask students to think about a famous person and to jot down two or three adjectives to describe him or her.

7 Elicit from the students the range of people they have thought of. Select one you think might inspire a variety of attitudes and emotions. Then take suggestions for suitable adjectives describing that person. Write them on the blackboard. Ask students to decide which are positive and which are negative and whether some are neutral.

8 Having introduced the idea of attitude, ask students to look back at their own lists and decide which words fit which categories: positive, negative, neutral. Elicit some of these and add them to the blackboard chart, explaining as you do so.

9 Give out copies of the quotations about Ghandi and ask students to decide what impression each of the possible adjectives gives.

10 Ask students to choose a famous person and to find out as much as possible about him/her. Then they should use their findings to write a short biography for the class magazine.

TASK SHEET   **Details needed for a biography**

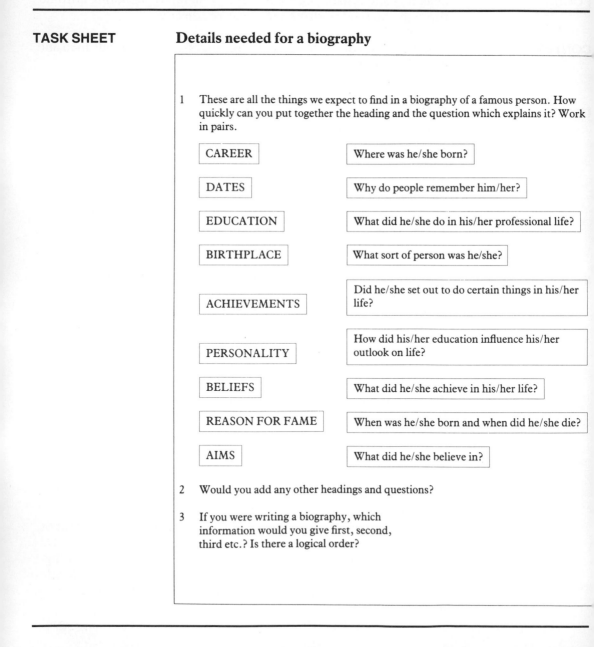

1   These are all the things we expect to find in a biography of a famous person. How quickly can you put together the heading and the question which explains it? Work in pairs.

CAREER	Where was he/she born?
DATES	Why do people remember him/her?
EDUCATION	What did he/she do in his/her professional life?
BIRTHPLACE	What sort of person was he/she?
ACHIEVEMENTS	Did he/she set out to do certain things in his/her life?
PERSONALITY	How did his/her education influence his/her outlook on life?
BELIEFS	What did he/she achieve in his/her life?
REASON FOR FAME	When was he/she born and when did he/she die?
AIMS	What did he/she believe in?

2   Would you add any other headings and questions?

3   If you were writing a biography, which information would you give first, second, third etc.? Is there a logical order?

SAMPLE QUOTATIONS

rebellious
subversive
determined

> Gandhi encouraged his supporters to block roads and railways as part of a peaceful protest. These actions caused great problems for the British administration in India.

obstinate
resolute

> Gandhi decided to fast in order to influence Muslim and Hindu leaders to stop the violence which occurred after Independence. He fasted until he was close to death.Finally the leaders pledged protection for Muslims in India.

visionary
idealistic
romantic

> Gandhi's dream was for a world where there was equality between people and in which there would be no rich or poor, master and slave.

frugal
miserly

> Gandhi and his followers lived a very simple life with few material possessions.

NOTE: You may make photocopies of this for classroom use (but please note that copyright law does not normally permit multiple copying of published material).

3.13 Writing simple instructions

LEVEL **Lower intermediate upwards**

TOPIC **Hurricane warning**

FUNCTION Giving warnings.

FORM A public notice.

FOCUS Short simple sentences; imperatives.

CONTEXT The students are writing a public notice for English-speaking visitors to a country where hurricanes or other natural disasters are experienced.

PREPARATION 1 Bring to class a picture like the one on page 127, which shows the effects of a hurricane.
2 Also make copies of the public notice which contains warnings.

IN CLASS

1 Ask students to look at the picture first and to say what it shows. They may have different words to describe the phenomenon. Ask how many students have experienced a hurricane, or if they have any experiences of their own to retell.

2 Explain that they are going to give warnings on a public notice for English-speaking visitors to a country which experiences hurricanes. See if they can suggest a few general warnings and write them on the blackboard to show the different forms that are possible:

– *Stay indoors.*
– *Don't leave any windows open.*
– *Make sure you have a supply of drinking water.*

Depending on the level of your class, give them more complex structures too:

– *Don't be fooled if the 'calm eye' passes over.*
– *Don't drive unless it is necessary.*

3 Ask students to think of warnings before, during, and after the hurricane. Give out the incomplete poster which gives them some ideas. Put the students in small groups to do this task so that they can pool ideas. You may need to prompt some ideas, as below:

Before *Have a flashlight ready.*
      Make sure you have a first-aid kit.
      Put batteries in your radio.
      Put the fire extinguisher somewhere handy.
      Put away all loose objects.
      Board up all the windows.
      Get away from low-lying areas which may flood.

During *Listen to your radio for advice from the authorities.*
      Keep your family together.
      Don't let any animals run out of the house.

After *Be careful with falling objects and broken glass.*
      Check for broken power lines.
      Make sure there are no fire risks.
      Use the phone only for emergencies.

4 When groups have completed the task, get them to read out the warnings to see if other groups understand them.

5 A useful follow-up task for homework is to ask individual students to devise a similar public notice for a situation which may occur in their own country, such as a forest fire, floods, earthquake, avalanche, etc.

Hurricane

Keep your radio or TV on and listen to the latest weather report to save your life and your possessions

Before the wind and flood
Have the gas tank filled in your car.
Check the battery and tyres.
Make sure you have a supply of drinking water.
Stock up on foods that need no cooking or refrigeration.
....
....
....
....
....
....
....

During the storm
Stay indoors.
Don't be fooled if the 'calm eye' passes over.
Don't be in the open when the winds resume.
....
....
....

After the storm has passed
Do not drive unless it is necessary.
Report broken sewer pipes.
....
....

YOUR ABILITY TO STAY CALM AND COPE WITH EMERGENCIES WILL INSPIRE OTHERS

NOTE: You may make photocopies of this for classroom use (but please note that copyright law does not normally permit multiple copying of published material).

3.14 Explaining purposes in instructional information

LEVEL	Lower intermediate
TOPIC	Is your house a burglar's dream?
FUNCTION	Giving advice.
FORM	A brochure or information leaflet.
FOCUS	Explaining purposes.
CONTEXT	The students are members of a local Residents' Association. They are designing an information leaflet giving advice to house owners in their area about how to make homes safe from burglary.
PREPARATION	Make copies of the picture on the opposite page.
IN CLASS	1 Ask if anyone in the class has been burgled and let them say something about the experience. You may have a story of your own to tell.

2 Ask students what they do to protect their home against burglars. Elicit a few ideas. Ask them to say exactly why they do certain things, for example:

– *I tell the police when I go away so that they can check the house.*
– *I lock up the shed and the garage so nobody can get the ladders or tools to open windows and doors.*

3 Explain that they are going to write a leaflet giving advice to people in their local area. Give out the pictures. Ask the students to work in pairs and to discuss the various points indicated on the picture.

4 Hold a short feedback session and see how many ideas they can suggest.

5 Take one suggestion and show students how the advice can be explained through a purpose, using the *so* or *so that* form, for example:

– *Leave some lights on when you go out so that it looks as if someone is in.*

6 Ask students to design the information leaflet in pairs, checking with other pairs as they work to exchange ideas.

3.15 Explaining reasons in cause and effect arguments

LEVEL
:   **Intermediate**

TOPIC
:   **Why do women live longer than men?**

FUNCTION
:   Explaining causes and giving reasons.

FORM
:   A short composition.

FOCUS
:   Connectives of cause and effect and organizing an argument into primary and secondary points.

CONTEXT
:   Preparation for academic writing of essays and reports in which discussion of cause and effect, reason and result is required.

PREPARATION
:   Make copies of the list of suggestions opposite.

IN CLASS
:   **1** Introduce the idea of women's greater longevity by reading this short extract from a Social Studies book:

> There are statistical differences in the life-cycles of men and women. For example, in Britain, 106 boys are born for every 100 girls. But the mortality rate at all ages is higher for males. So among the whole population there are only 94 males for every 100 females.

2 Ask students to suggest reasons why women live longer than men. Elicit a few ideas and, as students try to express them, show them various ways of explaining reasons and results:

In most countries only men take part in military combat.

- *As a result,*
- *As a consequence,*
- *Consequently,*
- *So,*

    } many young men are killed in wartime.

- *Since*
- *As*
- *Because*

    } men often take on the main financial responsibility of keeping a family, they develop stress-related illnesses and die younger.

One reason why women live longer than men *is that* their bodies are naturally able to survive longer.

3 Give students the list of suggestions as to why women live longer than men, and ask them to discuss in pairs. Ask them to decide which are the most important reasons, which are only secondary, and which are not true, or irrelevant. They may wish to add others.

Why do women live longer than men?

1 Women's physical structure allows them to live longer than men.
2 Men take part in military combat in wartime and women do not.
3 Men enjoy taking part in much more dangerous sports.
4 Men have more financial and economic pressures.
5 Far more men work in heavy industry which can be dangerous to health.
6 Women do not take on dangerous jobs such as mining, building, etc.
7 Men do not manage retirement well and just 'give up'.
8 ....
9 ....

NOTE: You may make photocopies of this for classroom use (but please note that copyright law does not normally permit multiple copying of published material).

4 Hold a feedback session and write up the primary and secondary points on the blackboard to give students the shape of their argument.

5 Show students how they can distinguish between primary and secondary points by using language such as:

– *One of the most important reasons why . . .*
– *The main reasons why . . .*
– *There are other reasons, too, . . .*

6 Students are now ready to draft their writing.

3.16 Using logical connectors for describing effects

This task uses the technique of mind maps described in *Composing* (see task 1.3). The topic chosen is a controversial one and may not be acceptable in some cultures, but there may well be another social issue which fits the culture and the context set out below.

LEVEL   **Intermediate**

TOPIC   **The drug addict**

FUNCTION   Describing effects.

FORM   Extract from an information brochure.

FOCUS   Using logical connectors of result.

CONTEXT   Writing an information brochure for children in secondary school as a warning against taking drugs.

PREPARATION

1 You need to prepare the content of the task by providing ideas and information to help the students.

2 You can prepare these beforehand in the form of a mind map so that you can help students if they run out of ideas for the extract.

IN CLASS

1 The topic of drug abuse is best exploited after a local event or national news report has brought it into discussion. Explain to students that they are going to write part of an information brochure for young people warning against the use of drugs. Read them these opening lines from such a brochure:

> Drug addicts are people who become 'hooked' on hard drugs and cannot stop taking them. Plenty of drug addicts have said that if they had known the whole story from the beginning they would not have started. Would you open a medical box and experiment by taking some of the pills you found in it? You are not likely to be so stupid. So why take drugs? Life for a drug addict is very hard . . .

2 Students are going to finish the extract by describing the effects of drug addiction. Ask them individually to make a mind map of the effects of drug addiction. Give them a few minutes to do this.

3 Then take ideas from the students and make a 'class map' of ideas on the blackboard. It could look something like this:

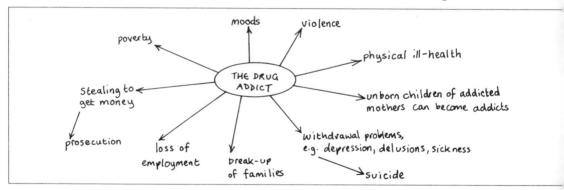

Figure 10

4 Continue the process of gathering ideas for the task by spending a little time on some useful collocations. Encourage students to think about the expressions they can use in the task by asking them to work in pairs to complete these lists:

- How many words can you make beginning with *drug* . . . ?
  (*drug addict, addiction, taking, etc.*)
- What kind of behaviour might a drug addict display?
  (*moody, violent, etc.*)
- What sort of problems can a drug addict experience?
  (*health, family, etc.*)
- What adjectives can describe the consequences of drug addiction?
  (*unhappy, tragic, etc.*)

5 Take one of the effects and show students the different ways in which this can be expressed.

Cause	**Effect**
Drug addicts can become very moody and sometimes violent.	This can lead to the break-up of families.
	One effect of this is that sometimes families break up.
	. . . as a result of which families often break up.
	. . . with the result that families sometimes break up.
	As a consequence, families sometimes break up.

6 Ask students to work in small groups for this task, arguing out the sentences they are going to write and checking with other groups.

REMARKS

Asking students to work in small groups on a short writing task has great advantages. It ensures a process of drafting and redrafting as students argue and try to improve their sentences. It enables weaker students to experience successful writing and to feel that they have contributed. It allows the teacher to monitor and give more help, as there are fewer pieces of writing in progress.

3.17 Organizing points for a contrast and comparison essay

LEVEL

Upper intermediate to advanced

TOPIC

Town and country life

FUNCTION

Contrast and comparison.

FORM

Composition of the examination type.

FOCUS

Discourse organization.

CONTEXT

Preparation for an examination question:
'The country has everything that is good in life; the city all that is bad.'

PREPARATION

In this activity you may wish to prepare the content needed for the essay as a list of points about town and country life. Make copies of the list for the students. These can be used for a matching and sorting task during the lesson.

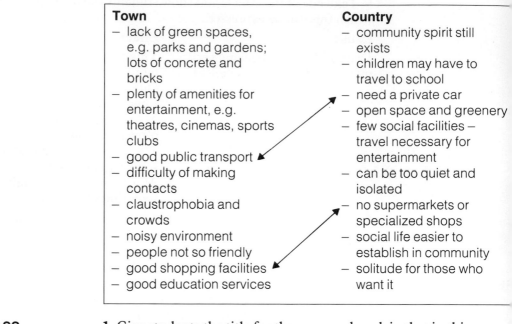

Town
- lack of green spaces, e.g. parks and gardens; lots of concrete and bricks
- plenty of amenities for entertainment, e.g. theatres, cinemas, sports clubs
- good public transport
- difficulty of making contacts
- claustrophobia and crowds
- noisy environment
- people not so friendly
- good shopping facilities
- good education services

Country
- community spirit still exists
- children may have to travel to school
- need a private car
- open space and greenery
- few social facilities – travel necessary for entertainment
- can be too quiet and isolated
- no supermarkets or specialized shops
- social life easier to establish in community
- solitude for those who want it

IN CLASS

1 Give students the title for the essay and explain that in this case the audience will be an examiner. They are to prepare a more formal type of academic composition.

2 Ask students to work for four to five minutes individually, jotting down ideas for the composition in the form of a mind map. You could start one together on the blackboard using the format below if students are not used to this kind of note-making activity (see also task 1.3).

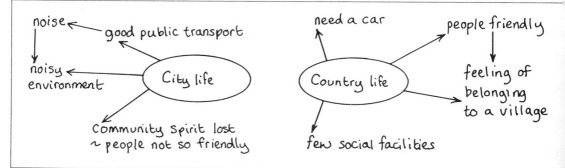

Figure 11

3 Elicit suggestions for content from the class and add them to the mind map on the blackboard.

4 Give out your copies of points for and against town and country. (This is a linear equivalent of the mind map.) Ask students to add any new points from the blackboard and any further points of their own.

5 Then ask the students to match points from each column which relate to the same topic (as shown by the arrows in the list above). This can be done individually or in pairs.

6 While checking the matching task with the whole class, discuss labels for the topics which have been identified: environment, social amenities, transport, etc.

7 Working with the class, decide on a sensible order for the topics. Looking back at their mind maps and any links between ideas may suggest ways of linking the topics together.

8 The next step is to show students a possible organization for their composition. As this composition involves quite a number of topics, an 'interwoven' organization is appropriate. It can be shown by drawing a diagram as follows:

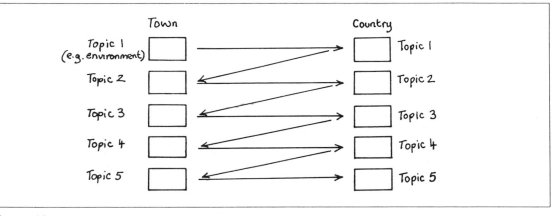

Figure 12

9 Students can then move to the process of drafting.

REMARKS Planning for a contrast and comparison composition is particularly important for two reasons. The first is that, in thinking about the topic, ideas occur randomly and must be related and organized in a logical way. Secondly, the content is complex and its organization needs to be worked out before drafting starts and the student begins to think about language as well. For this reason, in the task above, the students are given a chance to 'get their ideas together' through making mind maps. The move to linear notes helps them then to sort out the overall discourse structure.

3.18 Reformulating a paragraph

The following task is intended to help students understand the relationship between different sentences in a paragraph. It focuses their attention on the functional framework of a paragraph within a whole text. It then asks them to reformulate the paragraph in a slightly different way. As they do this, they will have to consider both the logical development of the ideas and the ways in which ideas are linked together through cohesive devices.

LEVEL	**Upper intermediate**
TOPIC	**Renewable energy**
FUNCTION	Review as part of an argument.
FORM	Extract from a brochure which seeks to inform and persuade.
FOCUS	Developing information through a paragraph.
PREPARATION	You need to make copies of the text and the task sheet.
IN CLASS	1 Take the title of the text, 'Renewable energy', and write it on the blackboard. Ask students to explain what it means and to give examples of some kinds of renewable energy. Ask them if they know what the source of energy is in their own home.
	2 Ask students to read the first three paragraphs of the text and to make a list of all the types of energy source that are mentioned. Check through these.
	3 Ask the students to work in pairs. They are to read the last paragraph and do the first part of the task together.
	4 Check through the numbered sentences of the task with the class.
	5 Ask them individually to try the second part of the task. When they have drafted out their own paragraphs they can compare with partners and see what differences there are. They can also comment on and suggest improvements to the first draft.
	6 It can be very useful for a later lesson to photocopy some of the completed paragraphs and to discuss with the class the different cohesive devices they have used.
TEXT	Read the text and then do the task that follows it.

renewable energy

The sun is the source of all life on earth and provides us with almost all the energy we use. Fossil fuels, such as gas, oil, and coal, are simply stored solar energy: the product of photosynthesis millions of years ago; while the renewable energy sources, solar, wind, tidal, wave, biomass, and hydro are all the direct result of the sun's energy.

More energy arrives at the earth's surface in an hour than is consumed in the world in a whole year. Even in cloudy northern countries like Britain there is more than enough solar energy for our needs. The total falling on Britain every year is more than one hundred times greater than all the energy used.

This energy can be used to heat buildings either directly (passive solar energy) or by use of solar collectors (active solar energy). The sun is also responsible for rain, which can be harnessed as hydro-power. Falling or flowing water generates 25% of the world's electricity. Waves are the result of winds over the ocean, and ways of harnessing this new source of energy are being developed at present, while the complex interaction of earth, moon, and sun results in the tides, which can also be used to produce electricity.

The official view in Britain is that renewable sources of energy such as these will be unable to provide more than a small proportion of our needs until well into the next century. But such pessimistic predictions are directly linked to the lack of money for research and development. In 1983/84 for example, only £11.3 million was spent on all the renewable sources of energy put together, while £206 million was given to the development of nuclear power. Some renewable sources, such as solar and wind energy, are already cost-effective and working well today. However, these are not being taken up by industry or the general public, due to lack of information on what is available, and financial incentives. We need to develop many of the more promising renewable energy options now if we are to ensure that the world has enough energy to take us through to the new century.

TASK SHEET

1 Look again at the last paragraph of the text. In what order does the author do these things? Write the sequence of numbers (1–6) in the boxes.

☐ Make a general statement of future needs.

☐ Describe the current level of development of renewable energy sources.

☐ Support an argument with an example.

☐ Give arguments against negative predictions.

☐ Criticize the official attitude towards development.

☐ Describe official predictions.

2 In what order would you do these things if you began the paragraph like this:

Some forms of renewable energy, such as solar and wind energy, are already cost effective and working well today.

Would you:
a. Decide on a general order?
b. Rewrite the paragraph and, as you draft it, decide whether you need to reword sentences or add anything in order to create a clear and convincing argument?

3.19 Organizing topics and points in an argument

LEVEL   Advanced

TOPIC   **An anti-nuclear power campaign leaflet**

FUNCTION   Giving opinions and justifying them.
                     Organizing an argument.

FORM   A campaign leaflet.

FOCUS   Organizing a set of arguments into a structure of topic, point, and evidence.

CONTEXT   The government is planning to construct a nuclear power station in a national beauty spot in an area in which the students live. They are writing a statement of protest from the Residents' Action Committee which plans to circulate a campaign leaflet in the neighbourhood.

PREPARATION

1 You will need to prepare the topic in terms of the kind of content which might be included in a campaign brochure and the way in which it may be presented. The extracts are designed to help you rather than to serve as a model for the student.

2 More specifically, you should prepare a set of slogans to write on the blackboard.

IN CLASS

1 Write on the blackboard a set of slogans against nuclear power stations, for example:

- RADIOACTIVITY ENDANGERS OUR HEALTH
- RADIOACTIVITY POISONS OUR EARTH
- NO NUCLEAR WASTE RISK
- WE WANT NO CHERNOBYL HERE
- PRESERVE THIS NATIONAL BEAUTY SPOT
- NO PLANNING WITHOUT LOCAL CONSULTATION

2 Ask students to work in pairs and to turn each slogan into a more detailed statement about the dangers of nuclear power stations.

3 When they have worked together for a while, hold a feedback session and ask students to suggest statements. Write them up on the blackboard. You may get something like this:

Radioactivity :

Nuclear Power Stations leak radioactivity into air, soil, rivers, and sea; pollute agricultural land.

Nuclear Waste :

Nuclear power stations produce wastes which remain radioactive for centuries.

Accident risk :

Nuclear power stations are a hazard; a serious accident in transportation or production can cause a major catastrophe. Loss of life ; increase in world radiation levels.

Destruction of natural beauty :

Ugly, unsightly buildings : radioactivity destroys natural environment for wildlife.

4 Show students how they can turn these statements into a series of arguments by following this pattern for each topic:

Topic	Radioactivity endangers our health.
Point	Power stations leak radioactivity into the air, soil, and water. As a result, radioactive matter can be taken into the body via food, drink, water, and air. It can cause cancer and genetic changes.
Evidence	More people, especially children, develop leukemia in the residential areas around power stations than in other areas.

5 Ask the students, in pairs, to construct paragraphs for each topic following this pattern, using a sub-heading for the topic, developing the argument by elaborating the point, and giving evidence to back it up.

6 When they have finished a first draft, ask students to think about the presentation of a campaign leaflet and to consider:

a. How would a real leaflet be organized?

– what kind of headings?
– how many sub-headings?
– how to begin?
– what kind of appeal to end with?

b. What style would be best for the readers and the topic?

– a direct style using 'we'?
– questions to catch attention?
  e.g. How long must we wait before the government comes to its senses?
– strong opinions?
  e.g. It is ⎱ essential that
        ⎰ horrifying that
          vital that

7 Ask students to take the first draft individually and redraft it to present a realistic leaflet.

EXTRACTS

NUCLEAR POWER
THE FACTS
THEY DON'T WANT YOU TO KNOW

If, like us, you thought that nuclear power would provide cheap, safe and abundant energy, then you, too, may be in for a shock. As we have discovered, the truth turns out to be rather different.

4.Q. Have there been any nuclear accidents?
A. THOUSANDS. MOST ACCIDENTS ARE NEVER REVEALED TO THE PUBLIC. At 3-Mile Island the near-disaster was caused - not by a single mistake - but by the sort of combination of technical and human errors which the nuclear industry has always claimed was impossible. Since 3-Mile Island the same type of valve in the same type of reactor failed at Crystal River, Florida - showing that the same impossible accident can happen twice. The U.S. government's Nuclear Safety Information Centre at Oak Ridge recently disclosed that of the 2,000 'incidents' investigated in 1979, no fewer that 32 might have ended in a catastrophic core meltdown - a fair indication of how close to the wind the nuclear industry sails. The British nuclear industry has categorically refused to publish its safety studies.

12.Q Can't radioactive wastes be safely disposed of?
A. NO: THE TECHNOLOGY FOR TOTAL CONTAINMENT OF RADIOACTIVITY DOES NOT EXIST. Some nuclear wastes remain radioactive for thousands of years. Wastes stored in tanks at Windscale leak unstoppably and those dumped in the deep ocean contaminate it. The really "hot" wastes are to be burned - maybe in your area. Instead of storing these wastes so that they can be monitored or retrieved for safer containment elsewhere should the technology for this be developed, it is proposed to bury them so that retrieval is impossible. They will certainly contaminate the ground water eventually, thus creating a genetic time-bomb.

25Q. What shall I do?
A. Talk to friends and neighbours. Tell them the FACTS. Remember: NUCLEAR POWER IS EXTREMELY DANGEROUS.   IT INCREASES UNEMPLOYMENT and produces expensive ENERGY OF THE WRONG KIND. Treat reassurances from the government and the nuclear industry with the utmost suspicion.
JOIN THE ANTI-NUCLEAR MOVEMENT NOW. If there is not yet a group in your immediate area, start one now. You will be surprised how eagerly people will join you as soon as they know the truth. Get your trade union branch, club or society to pass a resolution against nuclear power and send a copy to your M.P. Raise money for distribution of leaflets.
Leaflets: 100: £2.25   200: £3.50   500: £6.90   1,000: £13.00 Radiation leaflets at same price.
Posters: 10 assorted: £1.00   All prices include postage.
And/or send us a donation which enables us to give leaflets free to those who cannot afford to pay for them.
If you are interested in exploring in greater depth the points made in this leaflet and in knowing sources of information used, please send for pamphlet : 40p including postage .

3.20 Writing a book review

This activity can be started at the elementary level if your learners are borrowing books from a class library. You can provide an audience for the writing by displaying reviews in the classroom as recommendations for other students.

LEVEL	**Elementary**
TOPIC	**A chosen book**
FUNCTION	Writing a book review.
FORM	A short article.
CONTEXT	The students are writing a review of a book they have borrowed from the class library or resource centre in order to recommend it to their class-mates. The review will be displayed, along with others, in the book corner.

PREPARATION Put together materials from any well-known graded reader available to your students, and display them on the wall or in the book corner. As in the collage for the wall display, they could consist of:

– the front cover
– the 'blurb' from the back cover
– information from the title page
– an extract from the publisher's catalogue describing the series
– an extract from the opening of the story.

IN CLASS 1 Ask the students to work in pairs and to tell each other a little about a book they have read recently and enjoyed.

2 Bring the class together and ask a few students to say why they liked a particular book.

3 Write the words 'Comments' and 'Impressions' on the blackboard and remind students that this is one of the things we write in a review. We also need to include some background information. Ask students to skim through the information on *The Man Who Fell to Earth* and to note down the points they need for this background information:

– title
– author
– publisher
– simplified/abridged/retold/adapted
– fiction/non-fiction
– type of book, e.g. thriller, detective story, romance, etc.
– cover: comments on appeal
– illustrations, etc.

4 Then ask students to read the beginning of the story. How could they summarize this to give prospective readers an idea of the story?

Ask them to write a short paragraph summarizing the opening events. As they write, encourage them to look at each other's work. They might begin like this:

> The story begins in a small town in the USA. In the early morning a stranger . . .

5 With the class together, ask for suggestions as to what else might be included in a review. Build up a list of categories like the one shown under step 7.

6 Now ask students to write a review of a book they have read recently. The scheme for the review can be put up on permanent display in the classroom.

7 Reviews can be 'published' by asking students to read them aloud as recommendations or by putting them on display on the wall.

```
WRITING A BOOK REVIEW

  TITLE:        What is the title of the book?

  AUTHOR:       Who wrote it?

  TYPE:         Is it a detective story, spy thriller, horror story,
                historical novel, science fiction, romance, etc.?

  SUBJECT:      What is it about. e.g. family life, an unusual
                person, a mystery, an adventure?

  CHARACTERS:   Who are they? What are they like?

  SETTING:      Where does the story take place?

  TIME:         Is it written in the present time, or is it
                historical, or set in the future?

  EVENTS:       What happens? (Don't tell the whole story, just
                enough to interest your readers)

  IDEAS:        Is the writer saying something important about
                people? Is there a 'message' in the story?

  COMMENTS:     What was it like to read? easy/difficult?
                                            short/long?

                How would you describe the story?
                                    realistic? amusing?
                                    exciting? thrilling?
                                    fast-moving? sad?

                Did you like it?
                What did you like especially about it?
                How did you feel?  happy?  sad?
```

WALL DISPLAY

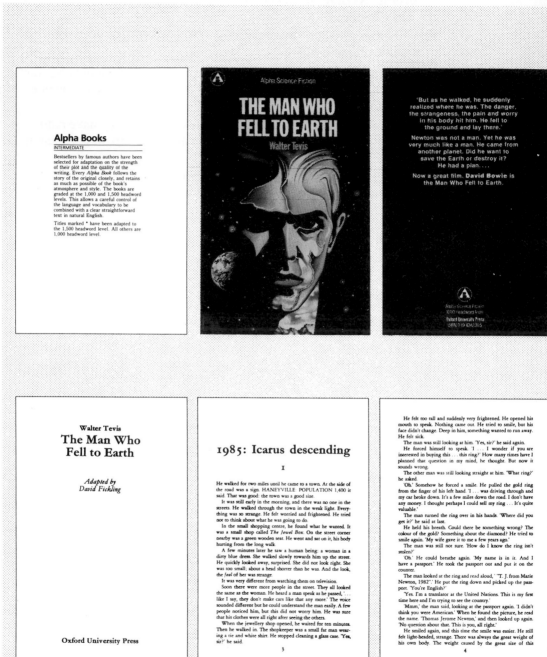

Alpha Books

INTERMEDIATE

Bestsellers by famous authors have been
selected for adaptation on the strength
of their plot and the quality of the
writing. Every *Alpha Book* follows the
story of the original closely, and retains
as much as possible of the book's
atmosphere and style. The books are
graded at the 1,000 and 1,500 headword
levels. This allows a careful control of
the language and vocabulary to be
combined with a clear straightforward
text in natural English.

Titles marked * have been adapted to
the 1,500 headword level. All others are
1,000 headword level.

Alpha Science Fiction

THE MAN WHO FELL TO EARTH

Walter Tevis

'But as he walked, he suddenly
realized where he was. The danger,
the strangeness, the pain and worry
in his body hit him. He fell to
the ground and lay there.'

Newton was not a man. Yet he was
very much like a man. He came from
another planet. Did he want to
save the Earth or destroy it?
He had a plan....

Now a great film. **David Bowie** is
the Man Who Fell to Earth.

Alpha Science Fiction
1000 headword level
Oxford University Press
ISBN 0 19 4242 31 5

Walter Tevis

The Man Who Fell to Earth

*Adapted by
David Fickling*

Oxford University Press

1985: Icarus descending

I

He walked for two miles until he came to a town. At the side of
the road was a sign. HANEYVILLE: POPULATION 1,400 it
said. That was good: the town was a good size.

It was still early in the morning, and there was no one in the
streets. He walked through the town in the weak light. Everything was so strange. He felt worried and frightened. He tried
not to think about what he was going to do.

In the small shopping centre, he found what he wanted. It
was a small shop called *The Jewel Box*. On the street corner
nearby was a green wooden seat. He went and sat on it, his body
hurting from the long walk.

A few minutes later he saw a human being: a woman in a
dirty blue dress. She walked slowly towards him up the street.
He quickly looked away, surprised. She did not look right. She
was too small; about a head shorter than he was. And the look,
the *feel* of her was strange.

It was very different from watching them on television.

Soon there were more people in the street. They all looked
the same as the woman. He heard a man speak as he passed, '...
like I say, they don't make cars like that any more.' The voice
sounded different but he could understand the man easily. A few
people noticed him, but this did not worry him. He was sure
that his clothes were all right after seeing the others.

When the jewellery shop opened, he waited for ten minutes.
Then he walked in. The shopkeeper was a small fat man wearing a tie and white shirt. He stopped cleaning a glass case. 'Yes,
sir?' he said.

5

He felt too tall and suddenly very frightened. He opened his
mouth to speak. Nothing came out. He tried to smile, but his
face didn't change. Deep in him, something wanted to run away.
He felt sick.

The man was still looking at him. 'Yes, sir?' he said again.

He forced himself to speak. 'I ... I wonder if you are
interested in buying this ... this ring?' How many times have I
planned that question in my mind, he thought. But now it
sounds wrong.

The other man was still looking straight at him. 'What ring?'
he asked.

'Oh.' Somehow he forced a smile. He pulled the gold ring
from the finger of his left hand. 'I ... was driving through and
my car broke down. It's a few miles down the road. I don't have
any money. I thought perhaps I could sell my ring ... It's quite
valuable.'

The man turned the ring over in his hands. 'Where did you
get it?' he said at last.

He held his breath. Could there be something wrong? The
colour of the gold? Something about the diamond? He tried to
smile again. 'My wife gave it to me a few years ago.'

The man was still not sure. 'How do I know the ring isn't
stolen?'

'Oh.' He could breathe again. 'My name is in it. And I
have a passport.' He took the passport out and put it on the
counter.

The man looked at the ring and read aloud, ' "T. J. from Marie
Newton, 1982." ' He put the ring down and picked up the passport. 'You're English?'

'Yes. I'm a translator at the United Nations. This is my first
time here and I'm trying to see the country.'

'Mmm,' the man said, looking at the passport again. 'I didn't
think you were American.' When he found the picture, he read
the name. 'Thomas Jerome Newton,' and then looked up again.
'No question about that. This is you, all right.'

He smiled again, and this time the smile was easier. He still
felt light-headed, strange. There was always the great weight of
his own body. The weight caused by the great size of this

4

3.21 Using connectors of concession

LEVEL	**Intermediate**
TOPIC	**A letter of complaint**
FUNCTION	Complaining.
FORM	A letter of a semi-formal kind.
FOCUS	Connectives of contrast.
CONTEXT	The students imagine they are adults who have watched a television drama with their children. The programme was scheduled early in the evening and it contained some violent scenes which upset the children. Knowing that the TV company has a policy of not showing violence until later in the evening, they write a letter of complaint.
PREPARATION	Make copies of the letter and the accompanying task sheet.
IN CLASS	1 Introduce the topic by asking students if they think that TV companies should have a policy on showing scenes of violence. Ask them to suggest guidelines.

2 Hand out the letter and the task sheet. Ask students to read through the letter quickly and to explain why the writer is complaining. Do they sympathize with her?

3 Draw the students' attention to the sentence beginning:

'In spite of . . .'

and explain that there are several ways of writing this. Elicit from the class the correct ways to complete the sentence frames.

4 Ask the students to use the structure and to choose a particular way of connecting the ideas from the examples shown. They should write one of the following letters:

a. Write to an English school you visited in the summer and which has still not sent you a certificate of attendance. They said they would send it within a week and it is now a month later.

b. Write a letter to your local Council. They said that a pile of rubbish outside your house would be taken away. That was two months ago.

REMARKS	Working with sentence frames like this can be a very effective way of showing the use of connectives and the grammatical constraints working on them. But it needs to be done in context, even if the letter is only a short one. This makes the task meaningful and the different structures are much better remembered.

EXAMPLE LETTER

Dear Sir,
I am writing to complain about the programme
'Harry's Place' which was shown on channel 5
last Thursday. In spite of your published
promise not to show unsuitable programmes for
children early in the evening, this was shown
at seven o'clock, a popular time for younger
viewers.

The programme showed a man pushing a young
child off a bridge into the river below. This
kind of violence is unforgivable. My children
were frightened and it was difficult to explain
it to them.

Yours faithfully
Jane Sinclair

TASK SHEET

```
1 ......................However..........................

2 Despite...............................................

3 ..................... yet...............................

4 Although..............................................

5 .....................Nevertheless.....................
```

*NOTE: You may make photocopies of this for classroom use (but please note that copyright law
does not normally permit multiple copying of published material).*

4 Improving

Introduction

This chapter is called *Improving*. The word describes the purpose of three different but related activities. The first of these is *marking*, traditionally regarded as the responsibility of the teacher. It often forms a considerable part of the work-load of the average English-language teacher. It usually takes place under pressure of time, and leaves teachers with a dissatisfied feeling that they can only make a minimal contribution to the improvement of an individual student's writing. The second activity is *redrafting*, the process that good writers go through as they evaluate, rethink, and rewrite parts of their texts. The third activity is *editing* at the post-writing stage, which involves checking for accuracy and making the final revisions.

The thrust of the argument in this chapter is that these three activities should be closely linked. In other words, that marking is maximally effective in enabling students to improve only if it provides constructive feedback which can be channelled into the processes of redrafting and editing.

How can we best help our students to improve their writing? In order to find answers to this, I think we need to ask and answer two further questions:

a. *What* are we looking for when we mark our students' writing?
b. *How* can we help our learners to see how their writing is improving and can be further developed?

The first part of this section will look at *what* and the second part at *how*. Task 4.1 relates to the *what* and tasks 4.2–4.8 deal with the *how*.

What are we looking for in our students' writing?

When we look at a piece of writing in order to assess it, we should ideally be asking ourselves a number of questions. Is this a good piece of writing? What makes a good piece of writing? What skills do students demonstrate in their written work which show that they are on the way to becoming effective writers in English?

This takes us back to the idea of the good writer raised in the *Introduction*, and to the components of skilled writing ability which good writers seem to demonstrate. If we list these components we can derive criteria for marking in the way represented in the diagram below. The components are divided into two groups. The first group consists of the skills involved in the process of composing, that is, having a sense of purpose, a sense of audience, and a sense of direction. Together they might be termed 'authoring' skills. The second group comprises skills connected with 'crafting', that is, the way in which a writer puts together the pieces of the text and chooses correct and appropriate language.

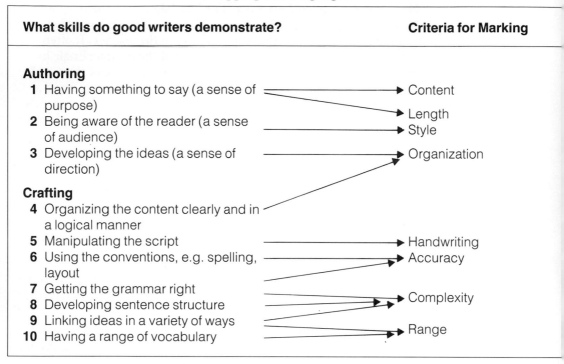

What skills do good writers demonstrate?   **Criteria for Marking**

Authoring
1 Having something to say (a sense of purpose)
2 Being aware of the reader (a sense of audience)
3 Developing the ideas (a sense of direction)

Crafting
4 Organizing the content clearly and in a logical manner
5 Manipulating the script
6 Using the conventions, e.g. spelling, layout
7 Getting the grammar right
8 Developing sentence structure
9 Linking ideas in a variety of ways
10 Having a range of vocabulary

Content
Length
Style
Organization
Handwriting
Accuracy
Complexity
Range

To take an example from the diagram, if we set up a criterion of complexity, it might relate to the ability to use complex sentence structures, which in turn requires an ability to use a variety of linking and co-ordinating devices and more complex grammatical structures. Similarly, a criterion of accuracy may relate to accuracy of grammar, spelling, punctuation, or conventions such as the layout of a formal letter.

The diagram is arbitrary and far from fully developed. It is simply meant to represent one possible method of generating criteria for the marking and assessment of writing. In this way teachers can formulate a checklist of components, select those which are appropriate to the age, conceptual development, and language development of their students, and derive suitable criteria.

One of the most interesting examples of such a scheme is the one produced by the Royal Society of Arts in its *Communicative Use of English*. This takes four criteria: accuracy, appropriacy, range, and complexity, and analyses degrees of skill at basic, intermediate, and advanced levels.

R.S.A. Communicative Tests

	BASIC LEVEL	INTERMEDIATE	ADVANCED
Accuracy	No confusing errors of lexis and punctuation. Grammar may be shaky but what the candidate writes is intelligible and unambiguous. Orthography may be uncertain.	Grammatical, lexical and orthographical accuracy is generally high, though some errors which do not destroy communication are acceptable. Handwriting is legible without undue effort.	Standards of orthography, punctuation, lexis and grammar are extremely high. Handwriting is easily legible.
Appropriacy	Use of language is broadly appropriate to function, though no subtlety should be expected. The intention of the writer can be perceived without excessive effort. Layout is generally appropriate.	Use of language is appropriate to function. Some adaptation of style to the particular context is demonstrated. The overall intention of the writer is always clear. Layout appropriate.	Use of language entirely appropriate to context, function and intention. Layout consistent and appropriate.
Range	Severely limited range of expression. The candidate may have laboured to fit what he wanted to say to what he was able to say.	A fair range of language is available to the candidate. He is able to express himself clearly without distortion.	Few limitations on the range of language available to the candidate. No obvious use of avoidance strategies.
Complexity	Texts may be simple, showing little development. Simple sentences with little attempt at cohesion are acceptable.	Texts will display simple organisation with themes and points linked and related.	The candidate demonstrates the ability to produce organised, coherent and cohesive discourse.

The most important aspect of a scheme like this is its *positive* approach to writing – one which looks for strengths as well as weaknesses. It is all too easy for marking to become a mechanical task of 'correcting errors' rather than a chance to indicate to students how they are developing as writers.

The criterion of complexity will serve as a good example of the importance of positive feedback. Students who are trying to develop an ability to write complex or compound sentences may well make errors in their choices of connectives, relative pronouns, or in the word order of subordinate clauses. If the only feedback they receive is negative, in the sense of corrections with no commendation for trying, they may well become discouraged and revert to writing simple sentences.

Students need positive feedback on the way their writing is improving, and this may be received through comments at the end of a piece of writing or through a grade of some kind. Attitudes to grading vary with educational systems and institutions, but if grading is the accepted norm then perhaps teachers need to review the system in use and decide on its merits and drawbacks.

Two examples of rather different grading systems are given on the next page, but each has the advantage of specifying to students the criteria upon which their writing is marked.

Grading criteria: Example 1

1 Organization of content (clarity, coherence, paragraph development)	20
2 Range (grammatical structures, vocabulary)	15
3 Complexity of sentence structure	15
4 Accuracy of grammar (tenses, agreement, etc.) of sentence structure (word order, connectives, etc.) of spelling of punctuation	30
5 Fluency (feel for the language, appropriateness, use of idioms, etc.)	20
	100%

Grading criteria: Example 2

	Excellent	Good	Adequate	Inadequate	Weak
A General development **1** Interest and force of content **2** Development of ideas **3** A sense of audience and style					
B Specific components in writing **4** Grammatical skills **5** Complexity of sentence structure **6** Use of vocabulary **7** Spelling **8** Punctuation **9** Presentation (neatness, handwriting, etc.)					

These examples are presented as sources from which teachers can develop systems appropriate to their own students. Many teachers prefer not to award grades but to use the simple strategy of writing comments at the end of a piece of work, though the latter can be time-consuming. However, a more detailed assessment is useful periodically, especially with motivated students who like to monitor their own development and assess progress in the various components of skilled writing.

It can be useful to involve your own students in the design of a grading scheme and in negotiating and prioritizing criteria (see task 4.1). This has the advantage of raising students' awareness of what makes a good piece of writing and, in multilingual classes in which students come from a wide variety of educational backgrounds, it prevents misunderstanding about the role and system of grading in your writing lessons.

How can we help our learners to see how their writing is developing and can be further improved?

The answer to this question lies, I think, in the degree to which redrafting, editing, and marking are linked activities. It depends on the respective roles of teachers and students in the process of revision.

In the majority of classrooms, the teacher may well be the ultimate arbiter of what is accurate and appropriate in writing, but this does not necessarily mean that final drafts must always be handed directly to the teacher for detailed and exhaustive marking. We have a number of alternatives in responding to written work, and these will largely depend on:

– the expectations students have of marking from their previous learning experiences
– the degree to which a particular error causes problems in understanding
– the personalities of individual students and the desire on the part of the teacher to build confidence, to discourage carelessness, etc.
– the marking load of a teacher and the time available
– the age of students and their ability to identify errors or cope with the technical language of a marking code
– the stage of writing development and the need to encourage students
– the aims of setting a particular piece of writing.

An increasing number of teachers are taking the view that correction 'after the event', when the writing experience is no longer fresh in the writer's mind, has serious disadvantages. Our alternative is to encourage as much revision and editing as possible during the writing process itself or immediately afterwards.

However, such activities only make sense as part of a much wider process of planning and composition. Students need to be sure that the 'global' structure of their writing is well organized before turning their attention to minor 'surface' features of word order, spelling, and so on. The concept and practice of revision should be very closely linked with the concept and practice of planning.

There is another major issue that has significant bearing on the effectiveness of the marking and rewriting process. When students are taught by a number of different teachers in a language school or department, or move from one teacher to another in a school system, the process of improving through correction, comment, and revision can only work well if there is a consistent methodology and scheme for marking throughout the institution.

It is not always an easy task to establish such a marking policy. Time is needed to thrash out the issues and form some kind of concensus on major issues. The following agenda for a staff meeting to discuss and design a marking policy might be a useful model for your own institution.

Questions for a staff meeting

```
1.What is the average marking load for
  one teacher in a week?

2.How much time do staff spend on
  marking?

3.What do students find helpful in
  marking?

4.What do students do with corrected
  work?

5.What strategies do/can/should teachers
  take towards marking?

6.What sort of comments do/can/should
  teachers write at the end of
  assignments?

7.What role does 'conferencing' play in
  the marking of work?

8.In what ways do/can/should teachers
  keep a record of each student's
  progress in writing?
```

Questions 3 and 4 are best discussed with reference to the opinions of students themselves. Student representatives could be asked to collect views, or a member of staff delegated to carry out an informal survey. The information thus gathered could be reviewed at the staff meeting.

If a marking policy is agreed by a team of teachers, then the institution might usefully consider publishing it as a document, so that teachers, learners, sponsors, and parents of younger learners can share an understanding of the criteria and procedures for correction, comment, and revision. A document such as the example shown below can be produced at different levels of language in English for intermediate and advanced students. For elementary students it is useful to translate it into their first language. It is a sensible strategy to create certain expectations in students at the beginning of a course about how their work will be dealt with, as this saves all sorts of misunderstandings later on.

A marking policy document

How your writing is marked in this school

1. First of all, you need to know that not all of your written work will be handed to your teacher for marking. Sometimes you will write in class and your teacher will read your work and help you as you go along.
2. While you are working, your teacher may start a discussion with you, asking questions, explaining things, and suggesting corrections or better ways of expressing yourself in English. The teacher may ask you to explain what you are trying to write or to evaluate what you have written. Join in the discussion. Its purpose is to help you learn.
3. When you have finished a piece of writing you should check it through to see if you can improve it or to find mistakes and correct them. Your teacher will give you some ideas about how to do this.
4. Sometimes you will be asked to check another student's work while he or she checks yours. This will give you practice in recognizing mistakes and will help you in your own work. Be as helpful and constructive as you can.
5. When your teacher marks a piece of work for you, do not expect all the mistakes to be corrected. Sometimes the teacher will tell you what is most important in this particular kind of writing, e.g. tense sequences in a story, and this will be corrected in particular.
6. When you get corrected work back from your teacher, read it carefully. There will be time to do this in class.
7. Sometimes the teacher will underline mistakes and ask you to try to correct them yourself. Sometimes you will find a note in the margin which suggests a better way to express something. Keep a record book of anything useful. Then you will learn from your mistakes.

Designing the policy itself involves making decisions about how to note corrections or suggestions for improvement on final drafts. One effective way of arriving at such decisions is for a group of teachers to mark some scripts together, discussing the options available. Alternatively, they could take sample scripts marked by different teachers and discuss the effectiveness of the marking strategies demonstrated. Possible strategies might be:

a. replacing part of the students' work with the correct form or with a more acceptable or appropriate version;
b. indicating an error by underlining and allowing the students to self-correct;
c. indicating an error and identifying the kind of error with a symbol, e.g. wo = wrong word order;
d. indicating that there is a certain kind of error on a line by writing in the margin but leaving the students to locate it themselves.

If teachers are going to use a marking code, then it is important that students are familiar with it. It could be displayed on the wall of the classroom on a handmade poster, or photocopied and handed to students. They will need time in class to work through a corrected script, understand the symbols and try to self-correct while the teacher circulates and helps individuals. Here is an example of one possible code. Try it out and see if it works for you. You may want to add other symbols.

WF	wrong form:	the <u>best</u> will be its achievements ^WF^
WW	wrong word:	patient, funny and <u>kindly</u> ^WW^
T	wrong tense:	In the last few weeks you <u>didn't have</u> much fun
∧	something is missing:	You arrived in Brighton ∧ the 1st
Sp	wrong spelling:	<u>con</u>fortable ^Sp^
WO	wrong word order:	You haven't seen [yet] London
P	wrong punctuation:	Look out. ^P^
V	wrong verb form:	The Titanic <u>sunk</u> very quickly
//	new paragraph needed:	
∅	not necessary:	John came in and (he) sat down
∪	You don't need a new sentence. Join up the ideas.	
?	I don't understand what you're trying to say.	
∿∿∿	This isn't quite right: it needs clearer expression (usually the teacher provides an alternative)	
[ ]	This part needs to be re-arranged or reworded.	
!!	You really should know what's wrong here because – we've just done it in class. – I've told you so many times.	

There is the question, too, of who designs the code. This one was designed with a group of upper intermediate students. It evolved from discussions of problems in writing and what to look for when trying to improve work after planning and writing a first draft. It was part of the process of raising consciousness about writing. Students and teacher suggested, negotiated, and agreed items, tested out the scheme and added to it. One of the additions was my own double question mark, used cautiously where students seem to know correct forms but are being careless. It was 'published' as a reference photocopy for each student in the group.

The rest of this section is devoted to a set of activities which show how students can be encouraged to improve their own work through self-correction strategies, exchanging work, conferencing between teacher and student, group writing, proof-reading exercises, class discussion of selected drafts, and reformulation procedures. All of these activities will be most effectively exploited where both teachers and learners understand the criteria and procedures for marking, revising, and editing.

4.1 Designing a grading scheme

LEVEL

Intermediate to advanced (or lower if carried out in the first language)

TOPIC

Marking compositions

PREPARATION

1 You need to have marked a set of scripts from your class, underlining weaknesses, etc., but you will not have graded the work or written comments.

2 You can build up the grading scheme on the blackboard or you can copy the task sheet and hand out copies for pair work.

IN CLASS

1 Hand back the marked scripts to your students.

2 Tell students that you are going to ask them to assess their own work. Elicit criteria for marking from the class by asking what makes a good piece of writing. Students will certainly produce some good ideas and you can suggest others. Build up a list on the blackboard.

3 Ask students to work in pairs and to prioritize the list on the blackboard or on the task sheet. Follow up with a class discussion to see if there is agreement about what is most important in writing.

4 Ask the class to use the criteria to write comments on their own essays and to award a grade.

TASK SHEET

Marking compositions

1 What do you think is most important in a composition? Put these things in order of importance (number them 1–10).

☐ correct grammar
☐ length
☐ originality of ideas
☐ spelling
☐ punctuation
☐ neat handwriting
☐ a good range of vocabulary
☐ complex and well-structured sentences
☐ good organization with introduction, body, and conclusion
☐ keeping to the title

2 Is there anything missing from the list?

3 Find out from your teacher whether his/her criteria are:

    a. the same as those listed here;
    b. the same as your own.

4 What kind of grading system do you think is best?

    a. double (a figure + a letter) for content and language;
    b. single – a percentage out of 10;
                 – a grade.

5 Now use the criteria and the grading system to mark your essay.

4.2 Conferencing

The writing conference is a face to face conversation between the teacher and student. As students work on their writing in the classroom, the teacher can sit beside one and talk about writing in progress, give support with organization of ideas, assist with the language, and extend the students' thinking about the topic, where this is relevant with young adults or with a specialized content. Conferencing encourages students to think about writing as something that can be organized and improved and gives them an opportunity to talk about their writing and reflect on the process. It gives teachers a chance to listen, learn, and diagnose. Florio-Ruane and Dunn (1985) usefully sum up the advantages when they say:

> By listening to the student and reading the work in progress, the teacher can come to know the . . . author's intentions, resources, growth, and needs. For the student, talking with a teacher about the work and responding to thoughtful questions is a way to expand and clarify thinking about audience and purpose as well as a moment to receive technical assistance and advice.

| LEVEL | **Intermediate** (or lower if you carry out the conference in the students' first language) |

LEVEL — **Intermediate** (or lower if you carry out the conference in the students' first language)

TOPIC — **A review**

PREPARATION — Prepare a guide such as the one on writing a book review (see task 3.20), and make copies, one for each student. No other preparation is necessary, as you will be working with the student's scripts.

IN CLASS —
1 Begin with a class discussion in which students suggest categories for comment in a review of a piece of literature. Write these up on the blackboard and suggest possible logical orders for information and review.

2 Give out the guide for writing a review, stressing that these categories could combine in many different ways.

3 Ask the students to discuss the questions in pairs to build up ideas for content.

4 In a short feedback session, encourage the class to discuss the questions, share ideas, write up language generated in the pair work, and check on ways of explaining literary features (consolidating earlier work).

5 Set students the task of writing an individual review of a piece of literature, using the guide in any way that might be helpful to them.

6 Begin conferencing with individual students after they have been writing for about ten minutes.

4.3 Raising awareness about writing

LEVEL — **Intermediate to advanced.** In monolingual classes with a teacher who understands the first language, the questionnaire can be translated for use at lower levels.

TOPIC — **A questionnaire on writing**

PREPARATION — Design a questionnaire which is most appropriate for your students. You may wish to use the one overleaf. Make sufficient copies for every member of the class.

IN CLASS —
1 Explain to students that you are going to ask them to think about writing in English lessons and that you are going to give them a questionnaire to answer.

2 Ask the students to tick those statements on the questionnaire which are true for them.

3 Put students in pairs and ask each pair to go through the questionnaire and explain their answers, developing and justifying what they ticked.

4 Take some of the statements to stimulate class discussion about writing and marking, and explain the kinds of activities you will set up during the course to help students to write, and tell them what your own strategies for marking will be.

REMARKS

As a class activity at the beginning of a course with intermediate to advanced students, this has several advantages. It encourages students to think about their writing, its state of progress, its strengths and weaknesses. It raises awareness in students of their possible roles and responsibilities in relation to the teacher's. It gives the teacher insights into the needs of students, their perceptions of writing, and their expectations of the course and the teacher. It also (and teachers need to make a mental note of this) obliges the teacher to negotiate a marking policy with the students.

SAMPLE QUESTIONNAIRE

What do you think about your writing?

Tick any of the statements below which are true for you. Then join in a class discussion.

1 I think writing in English is more difficult than speaking. ☐
2 I think I don't really have many problems in writing English. ☐
3 I don't write very much in my first language. ☐
4 Writing is important to me because:
  – I may have to write English in a job. ☐
  – I have to pass examinations in English. ☐
  – I want to write letters to English friends. ☐
  – .... ☐
  – .... ☐
5 I expect to do a lot of writing in class. ☐
6 I expect to do a lot of writing by myself at home. ☐
7 I would like the teacher to look at my work and help me while I am writing in class. ☐
8 I would like my teacher to talk to me about my writing sometimes. ☐
9 I usually check through my writing before I hand it in. ☐
10 I expect the teacher to mark *all* of the mistakes in my work. ☐
11 I expect the teacher to mark the most important mistakes in my work. ☐
12 I want my teacher to write comments about what is good or not good in my writing. ☐
13 I make a careful note of the teacher's corrections when I get work back. ☐
14 I usually read the comments and look at the grade but I don't study the corrections in detail. ☐
15 I would like to see other students' writing sometimes. ☐

4.4 Correcting your own work

It is a good idea, when students do their first individual written assignment for you, to leave time to talk about reading through and revising, to give advice about what to look for in their own writing, and to *show* them an example of a revised script. Experience shows that it helps students to get the idea of revision if they can actually see how another student has marked up a script for revision.

LEVEL   Intermediate to advanced

TOPIC   Revising strategies

PREPARATION   Collect examples from your students' work of drafts marked for
revision by writers (or by writers and you working together), or
make your own example. Photocopy sufficient numbers for each
student to see one. Alternatively, paste examples to a wall chart for
display.

IN CLASS   1 While students are preparing their first piece of 'in class' writing,
circulate and monitor the writing, making suggestions for
improvement and corrections. When you have looked at one piece
of work, tick the margin where you finish so that you can continue
from there next time round.

2 When students are nearing the end of the time for writing, stop
them and ask them to check through their work to try to make
improvements. Explain that it is difficult to write everything down
perfectly the first time and that professional writers always revise
and edit.

3 Make a list on the blackboard of things they can look for in their
own writing (much of this can be elicited from students'
perceptions of their own weaknesses):

– spelling and punctuation
– rewriting sentences to get word order correct
– linking sentences or ideas with connectives
– adding extra sentences to make the meaning clear.

4 Circulate while students revise their work, giving help and
advice.

REMARKS   Students usually find a number of mistakes in their work, or ways
of improving it. And with the teacher's help, a good deal of
effective revision can be undertaken. A possible drawback is that
students are too enthusiastic or become confused and begin to make
unnecessary corrections. Many teachers report, however, that
students build up a capacity to identify problems in their writing
and benefit from this process.

4.5 Writing in a group

LEVEL   **Lower intermediate to advanced**

TOPIC   **A story or description**

IN CLASS   1 Prepare a piece of writing with your class in the normal way. A
story or a description, e.g. of a festival, are the best types of text to
prepare, as these lend themselves to group writing.

2 Explain to your students that they are going to do this piece of
writing in a group, planning together, writing a section each, and
checking each other's drafts.

3 Organize your students into groups of four or five and appoint a group leader whose role is to get things started and to direct discussion.

4 Each group decides how to organize the writing, what the order of events (or parts of the description) will be, and how many paragraphs to write. Each student is to write one section.

5 When the various parts are completed, students exchange their work with other members of the group and mark the drafts for revision. They could be given a marking code like the one in the introduction to this section.

6 Students then redraft their work.

7 The various pieces can then be assembled and changes made to ensure coherence between them, such as careful use of time adverbials in a story.

REMARKS

This activity has advantages for both the teacher and the students. The teacher has six rather than thirty pieces of writing to monitor and assist with and can spend more time on the final drafts. The students gain help from each other in planning and drafting, and obtain experience in identifying problems in writing. Discussion by several people means that more ideas and improvements are applied to each piece of writing and the discussion itself can constitute natural fluency practice.

4.6 Pair-work editing

LEVEL

Elementary to advanced (Elementary students in a monolingual class could do this activity in their first language, and its essential value for writing development would not be eroded. Intermediate to advanced students could carry out the pair-work in English.)

TOPIC

Revision of a partner's draft

PREPARATION

1 Prepare a piece of writing with your class in the normal way.

2 Explain to your students that they are going to work in pairs, correcting and helping with each other's work.

3 Encourage students to talk about ideas for their writing with each other and to read bits out to their partner while they are writing.

4 When they have finished writing their first drafts, they should hand it to their partners, who mark the work and write comments.

5 Students then talk each other through the revisions and comments, applying to you for clarification or arbitration when necessary.

6 When students are satisfied with their own writing they can write a final copy.

REMARKS

This activity has several advantages. The editing takes place immediately after the writing, which makes it meaningful and useful to the writer. Practice in suggesting corrections in their classmates' work helps students to recognize errors in their own. When students have to explain points to a partner, their own understanding is redefined and clarified. It requires them to think carefully about clarity and acceptability in writing.

4.7 Reformulating

Reformulating is a valuable technique which makes revision and editing an integral part of writing classes. It moves away from the narrower idea of 'correction', which often tends to focus on the surface features of language, and gives students a chance to analyse and discuss the organization of meaning in their own writing and that of fellow students.

The steps given here are those suggested by Maggie Charles in a paper given at Brighton IATEFL, 1986, as a variation on the technique outlined by Richard and Joan Allwright (TESOL, 1984). The technique is ultimately derived from the work of Cohen (1983).

LEVEL

Upper intermediate to advanced

TOPIC

Any topic

IN CLASS

1 Students carry out a common writing task of a guided nature. You provide information so that students can focus on techniques rather than content. Task 3.17 is a good example of this.

2 Ask the students to discuss in pairs or groups a plan for the writing – how to organize the sections, order of information, etc.

3 Each student writes a first draft and gives it to you.

4 You 'mark' the work, i.e. proof-read it and indicate the main problems by underlining or using a system of symbols.

5 You 'rewrite' one student's essay, making sure you follow the ideas closely, but improving accuracy and appropriacy.

6 You then photocopy the original and the reformulation and distribute both to the class.

7 The class compares them, looking for the changes and discussing the reasons for them.

8 Students then go through their own draft essays and revise them to produce a final draft.

REMARKS

The advantages of reformulation are several. It enables students to see a 'native speaker' or 'proficient' model with which to compare their own attempts. It encourages students to discuss issues concerning overall organization, the development of ideas, the writer's sense of audience, and appropriate style. These important issues are often neglected in correction activities.

There is a risk, of course, especially when the technique is new to students, that they over-revise their own first drafts in an attempt to move towards the model, but this tendency decreases with greater experience.

4.8 Negotiating a reformulated script

The following variation on reformulation can be carried out with individual students, time and circumstances permitting. It is particularly useful with two kinds of learners: the learner with a lower level of language competence in a situation where teacher and student speak the same language and the discussion can be undertaken in the mother tongue, and the learner who has real problems in writing, and who needs individual help.

LEVEL

Intermediate (in English) and at any level if the discussion is undertaken in the first language.

TOPIC

A draft on any topic

PREPARATION

The activity is intended for one-to-one teaching, working on a script which the student has already drafted. It is probably a good idea, if the student has real problems in expression, to read through the script and get a mental picture of what he or she is trying to say.

IN CLASS

1 During the pre-writing stage, while students are thinking and planning, advise them to ask each other for help and encouragement, submitting their plans to each other for comment and helping each other with the language they need.

2 As you monitor the class, look over the plans that students are making and comment, provide language, advise, etc.

3 When the students have finished their first drafts, go through them yourself and reformulate the content in the way described in the previous activity.

4 Arrange to see the students individually. Go through the draft, presenting your reformulated sections, checking that you have interpreted correctly what the student is trying to express. Give the student every chance to explain, comment, evaluate the writing, and negotiate carefully the final reformulated version.

REMARKS

Few teachers can indulge in this kind of individual activity. However, it proves so popular and useful to students, it is worth trying to do it, if only once a term, with each student in the class.

5 Evaluating

Introduction

It seems appropriate, as the final point in a resource book for teachers, to devote the last section to evaluation. It provides an opportunity to summarize and review many of the ideas and issues explored in earlier sections.

There are two main reasons why teachers need to consider how writing tasks might be evaluated.

1 Making home-made materials
The first is that many teachers like to experiment with home-made tasks for their classes. Often, in the absence of appropriate materials for particular groups of learners, this is a necessity. However, it is also true for many teachers that the chance to design materials is an enjoyable and creative aspect of teaching. But classroom tasks should be designed with specific aims in mind, and we need criteria for evaluating whether those aims are likely to be fulfilled when students carry out the task.

2 Using published materials
The second reason is that the published materials we use regularly, or draw from occasionally in our classrooms, contain writing tasks of varying quality and usefulness. Teachers need ways of assessing the potential of these, and of predicting their effectiveness as teaching and learning materials. We need to ask questions like:
- Does this material encourage good strategies in writing, or do we need to add steps to encourage planning, revision, etc.?
- What aims does this activity have? Does it focus on a particular aspect of writing, e.g. paragraph development?

One useful approach to evaluation is to borrow a notion from the field of testing, *validity*, and apply it to materials (Ellis 1985). Firstly, there is the question of *internal validity*. This means evaluating a task in relation to its immediate and discernible aims and within the overall objectives of the textbook or set of learning materials. Most good, commercially produced textbooks, for example, come with an introduction or with a teacher's book which sets out the objectives of the book and even the precise aims of the activities within each unit of the book. We can therefore evaluate a writing task in terms of whether it fulfills the intended objectives of its designer.

However, this is only part of task evaluation. It is far more important for teachers to evaluate the aims themselves, in other words, to assess whether the task is *externally valid*. In order to do that we need to look at factors outside the materials themselves and decide whether they are likely to result in successful learning. This means considering such factors as the approach to writing implicit in task design, the suitability of the methodology involved to the expectations of our learners, and so on. Only then can teachers decide whether and when to use the materials and how to exploit them to their full potential by:

– working out a sensible sequence of steps for classroom use
– adapting elements of the task to improve it
– adding parts to bridge any gaps.

Applying evaluation criteria to sample tasks

The questionnaire that follows is designed to raise some of the key questions we need to ask and answer in the evaluation of writing tasks. It has five sections, each investigating an area of evaluation. These can be summarized as:

1 Aims
What form of written text, function of writing, and levels of writing 'skill' are in focus?

2 Approach
Does the activity place emphasis on process or product in writing? Is the approach one of modelling or creativity?

3 Motivation
In what ways does the task motivate the intended students:

a. through the subject matter?
b. through the methodology of the task?

4 Task design
What are the principles at work in the design of the task? What methodology is involved in its use?

5 Task adaptation
How could the task be adapted for most effective classroom use?

Each section has been elaborated into a set of questions which can be applied to any writing task. Try applying the questionnaire to the sample text that follows it, or to any other coursebook material you may be using. This might be a useful group activity for a teachers' meeting.

Evaluating writing tasks: a questionnaire

Aims

1 Does the task relate to an overall text type with a clear functional organization (e.g. narrative, description of a process, contrast and comparison, etc.)?
2 What form does the written work take (formal letter, postcard, composition, report, etc.)?
3 Which particular writing skills are in focus (logical development of ideas, use of cohesive devices in the text, or note-making as a way of planning writing)?

Approach

4 Does the task focus on product (i.e. how a text is organized or how the component parts are put together)?
5 Does the task focus on process (i.e. encourage students in effective and appropriate strategies for writing (planning, making notes, drafting, revising, self-assessment, etc.)?
6 Are students encouraged to follow model texts in producing their own written work?
7 To what extent can students use their own ideas, their own language resources to create texts?

Motivation

8 Does the material involve students as people, allowing them to exploit personal knowledge and experience?
9 How does the content of the task motivate (through relating to other curriculum subjects, widening cultural horizons, topics of universal interest, topicality, etc.)?
10 Does the methodology of the task motivate (problem solving or bridging an information gap)?

Task design

11 Has the context of the writing been made clear (if it is a description of a place, is it for a tourist brochure, a letter to a friend, or a geography textbook)?
12 Has the audience for the writing been made clear (a classmate, an organization, the school, an examiner)?
13 What is the degree of support and guidance given
  a. in the content (information, ideas, opinions)?
  b. in the language (vocabulary, structure, sentence construction, textual organization, etc.)?
14 What kind of classroom interactions are involved (individual work, classwork, pairwork)?
15 Has the task been carefully broken down into steps for students to follow?
16 Are the instructions clear and concise?

Task adaptation

17 Is there anything missing from the design? Can you see any problems with the task?
18 How would you adapt it for effective use with a particular class of students?

Sample text

5

Describing past events

Useful words
flat
gun
lock
police
police car
police dog
robber
robbery
break into
catch
fall over
fix
follow a scent
make a claim report
put *their* hands up
rob
search
telephone
turn upside-down
normal
tidy

Exercise 1
Imagine that you are the woman in this story and that your husband has just come home. Describe to him what happened.

Exercise 2
Now imagine that you are the policeman who looks after the dog. Write your report on this matter.

Exercise 3
You are the owner of the flat that was robbed in this story. Write to your insurance company, *The National City Insurance Company, 24 Old Street, London E.C.3.*, telling them what happened and giving them details of what you have lost and the damage done by the robbers.

Conclusion

In the *Introduction*, I began by saying that I hoped teachers would exploit the resources in a variety of ways, by adapting or adopting them as appropriate to learners. You may wish to evaluate the suitability of adopting a particular task for a certain group of students. You may need to adapt the task to another level of language competence. Or you may wish to take some of the ideas and adapt the content in order to create a task of your own. In all of these activities, as you exploit and extend the resources to suit your own teaching situation and the needs of your learners, I hope that the questionnaire for evaluating writing tasks may serve as a checklist of points for consideration in the design of motivating and effective classroom writing tasks.

Bibliography

L.G. Alexander	*For and Against.* London: Longman, 1969.
R. Allwright and J. Allwright	'Don't Correct – Reformulate'. Paper presented at TESOL, Houston, Texas, 1984.
British Council	Pair and Group Work in a Language Programme: A Film for Language Teachers. *Notes for Teacher Trainers* (prepared by Shelagh Rixon). The British Council.
Christopher Brumfit	*Communicative Methodology in Language Teaching: The Roles of Fluency and Accuracy.* Cambridge: Cambridge University Press, 1984.
Don Byrne	*Teaching Writing Skills.* London: Longman, 1979.
Maggie Charles	'Reformulation: Does it Work?' Paper given at IATEFL, Brighton, 1986.
A.D. Cohen	'Reformulating compositions'. TESOL Newsletter XVIII/6.
A. Davies and H.G. Widdowson	'Reading and writing' in *The Edinburgh Course in Applied Linguistics* Vol 3. Oxford: Oxford University Press, 1974.
Rod Ellis	'Lecture Notes and Student Worksheets for the Postgraduate Diploma in English Studies for Language Teaching'. London: Ealing College of Higher Education, 1985.
Susan Florio-Ruane and Saundra Dunn	'Teaching Writing: Some Perennial Questions and Some Possible Answers.' Occasional Paper No. 85. Michigan State University, 1985.
L. Flower and J.A. Hayes	'The cognition of discovery: defining a rhetorical problem' in *College Composition and Communication.* 1980.
Donald Graves	*Writing: Teachers and Children at Work.* London: Heinemann, 1983.
M.A.K. Halliday and R. Hasan	*Cohesion in English.* London: Longman, 1976.
Joint Matriculation Board	Test in English (Overseas)
R.B. Kaplan	*The Anatomy of Rhetoric: Prolegomena to a Functional Theory of Rhetoric.* Philadelphia: Centre for Curriculum Development, 1972.
Herbert Kohl	*Writing, Maths, and Games in the Open Classroom.* London: Methuen, 1977.
S.D. Krashen	*Writing Research: Theory and Applications.* Oxford: Pergamon, 1984.

Jerre Paquette   'The daily record' in *The English Magazine 9*. The English Centre, 1982.

Anita Pincas   *Teaching English Writing*. Macmillan, 1982.

Ann Raimes   'Anguish as a second language: remedies for composition teachers' in *Learning to Write: First Language/Second Language*. London: Longman, 1983.

Mario Rinvolucri   'Writing to your students' in *English Language Teaching Journal* 37/1.

W. Rivers and M.S. Temperley   *A Practical Guide to the Teaching of English as a Second or Foreign Language*. New York: Oxford University Press, 1978.

Harold Rosen   'Towards a language policy across the curriculum' in *Language, the Learner, and the School*. London: Penguin, 1969.

Royal Society of Arts   *Communicative Use of English as a Foreign Language*. London: RSA.

Mina P. Shaughnessy   *Errors and Expectations: A Guide for the Teacher of Basic Writing*. New York: Oxford University Press, 1977.

Frank Smith   *Writing and the Writer*. London: Heinemann, 1982.

L. Trimble   *English for Science and Technology: A Discourse Approach*. Cambridge: Cambridge University Press, 1985.

Ron White   *Teaching Written English*. London: George Allen and Unwin, 1980.

H.G. Widdowson   'New starts and different kinds of failure' in *Learning to Write: First Language/Second Language*. London: Longman, 1983.

Further Reading

Don Byrne   *Teaching Writing Skills*. London: Longman, 1979.

This is a practical handbook which begins with a consideration of wider issues such as the nature and purpose of writing and the particular problems it presents to learners of English as a foreign language. The book provides a wide range of controlled and guided exercises for different levels of language competence. It is particularly useful for its discussion of how to integrate writing with other skills work and how to organize a coherent writing programme from early to advanced stages of writing.

Susan Florio-Ruane and Saundra Dunn   'Teaching Writing: Some Perennial Questions and Some Possible Answers.' Occasional Paper No. 85. Michigan State University, 1985.

A useful paper which discusses issues of perennial concern to teachers, administrators, and policy makers in the field of teaching writing to mother-tongue learners. It raises interesting parallels for EFL/ESL teachers in investigating such questions as: Why is writing difficult to teach? What roles do teachers play in writing? What are the current problems and challenges of writing instruction in schools?

Aviva Freedman, Ian Pringle, and Janice Yalden	*Learning to Write: First Language/Second Language*. London: Longman, 1983. The themes of this book are wide-ranging: current research into the product and process of writing; the place of writing in the cognitive development of young learners; points for the design of writing tasks; classroom practice. It also spans the fields of mother-tongue, second language, and foreign language teaching of English, and discusses writing in relation to both children and adults. The book is divided into four sections: the writing process; the development of writing abilities; text and discourse, and implications for teaching.
Donald Graves	*Writing: Teachers and Children at Work*. London: Heinemann, 1983. Donald Graves has been studying young mother-tongue writers in school to find out what developing writers can teach us about the processes involved in writing. He suggests that his book is read as a collection of 'workshops' which offer advice on classroom practice and insights into the process of 'growth' in writing ability and the factors which influence it.
S.D. Krashen	*Writing Research: Theory and Applications*. Oxford: Pergamon, 1984. Krashen provides a brief but comprehensive summary of research into first and second language writing. He suggests that processes in both are similar and that the major problems for writers in both contexts are an inefficient composing process and a lack of acquisition of the code of written English. He goes on to discuss the link between reading and writing and to suggest how teachers might help developing writers. It is an accessible and informative book for those who wish to delve more into the 'theory' of writing.
Frank Smith	*Writing and the Writer*. London: Heinemann, 1982. Frank Smith offers a stimulating analysis of what writing involves for a writer and for a child learning to write. He explores interaction between the writer and the text and the reader/writer contract. The book is reflective and highly individualistic. It builds theories, but does not attempt to offer any analysis of data or observation of writers writing, nor to discuss certain basic issues such as the different functions of writing and the effect of this on texts. Nevertheless, the book is thought-provoking for teachers of writing in any context.
Ron White	*Teaching Written English*. London: George Allen and Unwin, 1980. A compact and accessible discussion of how to teach 'institutional' writing, that is, objective prose which conveys accurate and comprehensible information within the stylistic conventions of professional roles and institutions. It presents well-organized sections on narrative, description, etc. with useful examples, lesson plans, and teaching procedures. A practical and concise reference and resource book for the EFL teacher.